WALKING IN HIS WAYS

Spiritual Food
For Spiritual Growth

BOOK 2

NANCY TAYLOR TATE

Walking in His Ways

Spiritual Food for Spiritual Growth

Nancy Taylor Tate

First Edition

This printing September 2022

COPYRIGHT © 2022

Nancy Taylor Tate

Contact Information for Nancy Taylor Tate can be found on our ministry website:

www.wadetaylor.org

Deeper Life Press

Contents

Section 1: *Our Foundation* 11

  A Personal Testimony...11

  The Call of God 18

  In His Word I Do Hope 22

  A Hearing Ear 28

Section 2: *Divine Guidance* 34

  Abba Father 34

  But the Lord Said 45

  Watching at His Gates..................................... 54

  Urgency of Spirit... 57

  Staying Under the Cloud.................................. 61

Section 3: *Relationships* 66

  Beautiful Feet.. 66

  Crinkled Eyes.. 71

  Love One for Another.......................................77

  Love Perfected in Me...................................... 86

  Dwelling in Love 92

  Treasuring Our Relationships........................... 98

Section 4: *Forgiveness*...................................103

  Do Not Be Swallowed by a Whale! 103

  The Power of Forgiveness 110

  The Importance of Clear Vision...................... 117

  A Peace that Surpasses All Understanding 124

Section 5: *Managing Our Time*....................... 129

  Push Through or Stop?....................................129

Running on Empty 133

Preparation for Visitation 141

Pressing Through Busyness 148

Section 6: *Victorious Living* 154

Filled With Assurance 154

Living From an Eternal Perspective 160

A Triumphant Procession 169

The Fragrance of His Presence 176

Living Testimonies 181

Section 7: *The Faithfulness of God* 186

Faith of Our Fathers – Living Still 186

Encouragement 200

Living With Purpose 206

Maintaining Focus 211

Believing God 217

A Commitment to the Lord 222

Final Thoughts 226

Blessing 229

Appendix: *The Lasting Value of Communion* 230

Books by Nancy Taylor Tate 250

Acknowledgements

Thank You,

Lord, for Your faithfulness, love, and enabling grace

With appreciation,

I acknowledge and ask that You bless

Allen Tate, my husband and best friend, joined in heart, calling, life, and ministry

Sharon Whitby, my niece, who is an awesome editor and fun to work with

Steve Porter, our friend, who encouraged and helped us publish these books

Prayer Partners, Friends, and Family who have made a difference in my life

Dedication

I dedicate this book with love to Joe Wade, my son, and to his family

In Loving Memory of

David, my husband until the Lord took him home, for his love, faith, and prayers

Wade Taylor, my dad, for truths he shared, impacting my life and walk with the Lord

Section 1

Our Foundation

A Personal Testimony

"But we all, with open face beholding as in a glass the glory of the Lord, are changed into the same image from glory to glory, even as by the Spirit of the Lord." 2 Corinthians 3:18

Someone said to me once, "Nancy, who *are* you?" At the time, I didn't know if I should be flattered or insulted. We had worked together; I thought they knew me well.

But today, I smile. What they were sensing was a change in my life.

> *"Who is this that cometh up from the
> wilderness, leaning upon her beloved?"* Song
> of Solomon 8:5a

In my prayer closet, while under no pressure, I had been praying into and waiting on the Lord with scriptures and spiritual truths that He was making real to me.

Through the strength that was imparted to me during those times, I began to make choices, living and walking them out until it became no longer my choice but my very nature, as I grew in my relationship with the Lord and identification with Him.

Paul said:

> *"I am crucified with Christ: nevertheless I live;
> yet not I, but Christ lives in me."* Galatians
> 2:20a

What a wonderful experience as change begins to take place in our lives! I was brought into a succession of triumphs beyond what I had known in the past.

There are two aspects to our spiritual walk with the Lord Jesus Christ. The bridal aspect speaks of a loving relationship, our devotional times with Him.

Then as a son, I am to learn to walk in His ways. As I come under His headship, His working takes place in my life, bringing every aspect of my being into alignment with who He is.

> *"For as many as are led by the Spirit of God, they are the sons of God."* Romans 8:14

In this newfound union with Him, He invites me to participate with Him in that which He is doing, in a submissive relationship to Him, as His heart and life find expression through me.

> *"Come, my beloved, let us go forth into the field; let us lodge in the villages. Let us get up early to the vineyards; let us see if the vine flourish, whether the tender grape appear, and the pomegranates bud forth: there will I give thee my loves."* Song of Solomon 7:11-12

The first book of this series, *That I Might Know Him*, emphasizes the devotional aspect of our lives as we're brought into a deeper relationship with Him. In this deepening relationship, we find a meaningful and fruitful lifestyle filled with love, joy, peace, and purpose, through our union with Him.

This book, *Walking in His Ways,* emphasizes knowing His ways and learning to walk in them. As we do, we begin to meet the challenges of the day with the mind of Christ and His heart. This poise of spirit brings endless victories into our lives as the Lord Jesus Christ continues to work within us while He also impacts the earth and those around us.

What a glorious calling and life! His purposes being fulfilled in us and through us! I know of no better way of living, no greater source of joy or fulfillment. Whether I am single, married, widowed, or whatever state I'm in, the Lord fills my life and is my joy.

There is a void within each one of us that only God Himself can fill. From that place of wholeness, we are then free to grow in healthy relationships with others.

And what beautiful relationships the Lord blesses us with as we journey through this life! As the Lord joins us with others of like mind, and together we walk in this relationship with the Lord, what harmony, what joy it brings!

Good times or challenging times, may we never miss an opportunity for the Lord to be whom He wants to be and do what He wants to do, not only in our circumstances but in our hearts. May we join in the triumphant procession of an overcoming people, empowered by His Spirit, and being raised up for His end time glory.

> *"He made known his ways unto Moses, his acts unto the children of Israel."* Psalm 103:7

As His presence is being made manifest and His glory is being revealed, may we not just "see" the acts of God as the Israelites did. But may we come to "know" the ways of God, as Moses did. There is a difference!

> *"At the commandment of the LORD they rested in the tents, and at the commandment of the LORD they journeyed."* Numbers 9:23a

The Lord is looking for those who would become carriers of His presence and that which He is doing. Those who know Him and who know His ways. Those who are willing to move with Him and wait with Him as they learn to follow Him, always abiding under His headship. (See Numbers 9:15-23 for a fuller picture of this.)

When you approach the subject of the submission of our lives to the Lord Jesus Christ, some people step back, thinking of it as a hard way to live. But I have found it thrilling and fulfilling, liberating and joyful, an exciting way to live a victorious life, taking me on paths I never dreamed of.

Even as the Lord has brought me from victory to victory, may you too find increasing joy and purpose, a way of living that is fulfilling in this life, yet preparation for all that is ahead.

> *"For since the beginning of the world men have not heard, nor perceived by the ear, neither hath the eye seen, O God, beside*

thee, what he hath prepared for him that waiteth for him." Isaiah 64:4

Paul says it like this:

"But as it is written, Eye hath not seen, or ear heard, neither have entered into the heart of man, the things which God hath prepared for them that love him." 1 Corinthians 2:9

This book is best read devotionally, one chapter at a time. Each chapter is complete in itself. I encourage you to pray into the scriptures and truths that are shared as you continue reading.

God has a wonderful plan for each of our lives. My prayer is that through this book, you will be strengthened in your walk with the Lord. That you will not only increasingly recognize His ways but be empowered to walk in them.

The Call of God

"And he goeth up into a mountain, and calleth unto him whom he would: and they came unto him. And he ordained twelve, that they should be with him, and that he might send them forth to preach, and to have power to heal sicknesses, and to cast out devils." Mark 3:13-15

There are those who might think it's selfish to spend time seeking the Lord when we ought to be praying for others. We are to pray for others, but there is a basic principle: You can't give what you don't have! On an airplane, they say to put your own air mask on before you try to help someone else. We need to learn to do this spiritually as well!

Although there is much that could be said from the above verse, the principle I would like to focus on is this: Our primary call is to *"be with Him."* From that place of being with Him, all else will flow as He enables us to do those things He calls us to do. This key, found in verse 14, is sometimes overlooked.

"And he ordained twelve, that they should be with him, and that he might send them forth."
Mark 3:14

Someone once told me something my dad said and asked me why he said that. I did not know; I had never heard him say that. But I knew my dad, and if he did say that, I thought I knew why. Later I asked him if I was right, and he said yes. How did I know? I had spent time with him. I had come to know his nature, his way of thinking.

The Lord is calling today for those who would know Him on this level. He is looking for those who would respond to His call, that they might go forth in His nature and character, with His heart.

Ivan Q. Spencer said, "We must consider the reproduction of the Christ within His many-membered body and how we are neglecting this very important truth. We are not yielding fully to the Holy

Spirit to bring us into this truth because we are so occupied with service and other distractions.

We must realize that this is the hour of travail for the Church ... the birthing of the man child or the forming of Christ in us. God is laying His hand upon a body of overcomers and drawing them into a place of intimacy with Himself so that He can prepare them for the coming reign with Him."

What a calling! Christ *in* you, the hope of glory! (Colossians 1:27; 2 Thessalonians 1:10). Christ *in* us!

The foundation for this is a personal relationship with the Lord Jesus Christ. We must be born again (John 3:3,7; Romans 3:23; 1 John 1:9; Titus 3:5; 1 Peter 1:23). Then, as we spend time with Him, not only do we come to know Him more, but we are also changed. May we recognize and respond to the call to *"be with Him."*

From this place of intimacy, He will equip and empower us with divine enablement for all He has called us to be and do. May we set apart quality times to be alone with Him, that we might be strengthened to practice His presence every moment of every day as we become a part of those who *"follow on to know the Lord."*

> *"Then shall we know, if we follow on to know the LORD: his going forth is prepared as the morning; and he shall come unto us as the rain, as the latter and former rain unto the earth."* Hosea 6:3

What a beautiful promise ...

In His Word I Do Hope

"I wait for the LORD, my soul doth wait, and in his word I do hope." Psalm 130:5

I so appreciate my times of Bible reading and prayer. I may be reading my Bible, or my husband may be reading scriptures as we have coffee together. Other times I may be listening to scriptures through Alexander Scourby or others who have made recordings of Bible readings.

I also love to quietly hold scriptures in my heart as I sit in the Lord's presence or as I am doing chores. These scriptures that have become embedded in my heart and memory over the course of time, I can now set my thoughts on, or pray into, as the verses come to mind.

And I love scripture songs! What a beautiful way for scripture to get into our hearts as we listen to or sing the words! What an uplifting and encouraging way of worshipping the Lord!

In whatever ways we take time to linger in God's Word, how important His Word is in our lives. It is through God's Word that we have fellowship with the Father through Jesus Christ and the communion of the Holy Spirit. It is through God's Word we come to know His love and learn to trust Him.

We receive our daily spiritual food and find strength for the journey through His Word. The Lord is calling us up into a place of unbroken fellowship with Him as we learn to eat, think, and live His Word.

Psalm 119:105 says, *"Thy word is a lamp unto my feet, and a light unto my path."* Day by day, may we take time to spend time in His Word and in fellowship with Him.

May decisions we make be grounded in God's Word. As we pray, may it be God's Word going back to Him. May we be quick to have an encouraging word for someone else based on God's Word.

As we spend time in God's presence with His Word, it goes deep into our hearts. The Holy Spirit brings to remembrance the Word of God; that's His part. But it needs to be in there for us to remember; that's our part.

The Bible speaks of those who know the word of truth and rightly divide it:

> *"Study to shew thyself approved unto God, a workman that needeth not to be ashamed, rightly dividing the word of truth."* 2 Timothy 2:15

The Bereans were commended because they received the word readily, then searched the scriptures for confirmation.

> *"These were more noble ... in that they received the word with all readiness of mind, and searched the scriptures daily, whether those things were so."* Acts 17:11

Notice it is *especially* those who spend time in the Word who are considered worthy of double honor.

> *"Let the elders that rule well be counted worthy of double honour, especially they*

who labour in the word and doctrine." 1
Timothy 5:17

God's Word is light and truth. Through His Word we
are kept from error.

"And Jesus answering said unto them, Do ye
not therefore err, because ye know not the
scriptures, neither the power of God?" Mark
12:24

Through God's Word, we are spiritually edified and
receive spirit and life. Jesus said:

"Man shall not live by bread alone, but by
every word that proceeds out of the mouth
of God." Matthew 4:4

"It is the spirit that quickeneth; the flesh
profiteth nothing: the words that I speak unto
you, they are spirit, and they are life." John
6:63

Some seek to be led by the Holy Spirit without being
properly grounded in God's Word. Others look at the

letter of the Word without allowing God's Spirit to move through it.

Even as it takes two wings for a bird to fly, so it takes two wings – the wings of His Word and of His Spirit – if we are going to soar up into that place of fellowship and function that God is calling us into today.

May God's Word change us and bring us into the fullness of His purpose for our lives. His words are spirit and life, sharper than any two-edged sword, bringing conviction but also expectation and hope that we might be led on paths of righteousness.

"Thy word have I hid in mine heart, that I might not sin against thee" (Psalm 119:11). As His Word goes deep into our hearts, may it then find expression through our lives, that Jesus may be seen and glorified.

Whether we read, study, meditate, pray, sing, or declare God's Word, may He bless, strengthen, and encourage us today, and every day, as we take the time to spend time in His Word.

May we say with the psalmist:

"I will delight myself in thy statutes: I will not forget thy word." Psalm 119:16

"I wait for the LORD, my soul doth wait, and in his word I do hope." Psalm 130:5

A Hearing Ear

"Who hath ears to hear, let him hear."
Matthew 13:9

In Genesis 3:9, the Lord called out to man in redemption, "Adam, where are you?" The Lord had pronounced eternal judgement on the serpent; however, for all of mankind, God desired the reconciliation of man to Himself. The Lord sought a confession from Adam as the first step toward his redemption, because confession releases the blessing of God.

In the book of Revelation, the Lord is yet calling out to all those who would choose to submit their lives to Him, that they might enter into an active, on-going, personal relationship with Him.

> *"Behold, I stand at the door, and knock: if any man hear my voice, and open the door, I will come in to him, and will sup with him, and he with me."* Revelation 3:20

This verse often speaks to the heart of those who do not know Christ as their Saviour, that they might invite Him into their hearts and lives. Yet, in this context, it also has a message for the Church.

The seventh church, which is the last church mentioned in the book of Revelation, has become "rich and increased with goods," but blind to their own inner need. Here, in essence, the Lord is saying, "I am knocking on the door of your heart. Will you invite Me to come in, so I might sup with you? There is much that I long to share with you.

Are you listening? Do you hear? Are you willing for Me to come into your busy schedule for times of fellowship with you?

If you will respond, in My presence a door will open, that you might stand in the presence of My throne where you will experience My glory. But first, you must open the door for Me to come into your life in a more intimate way. You must make time to commune and fellowship with Me."

Abraham, who is referred to in scripture as "the friend of God," is an example of this principle and its outworking. In the heat of the day, as Abraham sat in the door of his tent, the Lord suddenly appeared. Abraham ran to meet the Lord and immediately began to minister to Him.

Abraham could have been preoccupied with the needs in his own life. He was old in age and had been promised a son, but there was no evidence of this promise being fulfilled.

Yet, when the Lord appeared, Abraham did not mention himself or his hopes and dreams. Rather, his entire attention was directed toward fulfilling the need of the Lord at that particular moment.

It was with this person that the Lord shared His heart: "Should not I tell Abraham that which I am about to do?" Thus, the Lord was able to use Abraham in intercession, that the righteous might be brought out of Sodom before judgment fell.

As a result of Abraham's intercession, the intervention of the Lord in that city was so powerful, that an angel literally took Lot by the hand and brought him out when he would have lingered. The Lord remembered Abraham and therefore was merciful.

Today, the Lord is looking for those with whom He might share His heart. He is seeking for those who will give themselves wholly to that which He is doing.

As we give ourselves totally to the Lord and to those things that are on His heart, the Lord will take care of all that concerns us, for the Lord loves those who love Him.

> *"I love them that love me; and those that seek me early shall find me."* Proverbs 8:17

Abraham did not have to ask the Lord again about his promised son. As Abraham put the Lord first in his life, the Lord, on His own initiative and in the fullness of His timing, fulfilled His promise to Abraham and gave him his promised son.

In the same way today, the Lord is knocking on the door of all those who have submitted their lives to

Him. He is seeking out those who have a listening ear and who desire to come higher in vision and purpose.

Yet many within the Church have become busy and satisfied with other things. There is a lack of intimacy of relationship that would cause them to actively look in expectancy for the presence of the Lord and the deep inner workings of the Holy Spirit in their lives. This has resulted in a dullness of hearing the voice of the Lord. They are satisfied with being saved, without a desire for more.

Paul cried out, "that I might know Him." He expressed his heart's desire to be made conformable to the Lord's death, that he might live with Him in resurrection life and power. As a result, Paul not only saw things unspeakably wonderful, but experienced this power in his own life and ministry as he was enabled by the Lord to live an overcoming life and experience "the fellowship of His sufferings."

Today, the Lord is calling and knocking. He not only is calling out in redemption to the lost, but He also is knocking on the door of all those within the Church, that they might respond and come to know Him in a deeper way.

The Lord is seeking out all those who have a burning desire to know Him, that He might make Himself known to them in greater ways. We have opportunity to know the Lord not just as an acquaintance or even a good friend; but as an intimate friend knows his friend, so the Lord would have us come to know Him.

May we be found among those who are "listening to His knock" and opening the door that will take us beyond all that we are presently involved in, into greater times of fellowship with the Lord.

Wherever you may be at this present moment, the Lord is knocking on the door of your heart that you might respond to His desire to more fully make Himself known to you.

May we have "an ear to hear."

Section 2
Divine Guidance

Abba Father

"I will guide thee with mine eye." Psalm 32:8

David wrote in Psalm 31:1, *"In Thee, O LORD, do I put my trust."* I have come to understand that the trust he is talking about is measured not only by warm feelings as we sing hymns in church on Sunday, but by the choices we make throughout the week. Those choices, and how we make them, are greatly determined by the inner posture of our heart.

A little prayer I pray sometimes is just two words, *"Abba, Father."* To understand what these words mean, think of a little child in his father's arms. That child is not afraid that his father might drop him. He is totally secure in his father's arms.

> *"And because ye are sons, God hath sent forth the Spirit of his Son into your hearts, crying, Abba, Father."* Galatians 4:6

In prayer, I sometimes spend time just focusing on the Lord and who He is, allowing trust to settle in my heart. The Word says that he who comes to God must believe that *"He is"* and that *"He is a rewarder"* of those who earnestly seek Him. As I hold this in my thoughts, I believe into these words and allow them to sink into my innermost being.

> *"But without faith it is impossible to please him: for he that cometh to God must believe that he is, and that he is a rewarder of them that diligently seek him."* Hebrews 11:6

Another verse tells us that God loves those who love Him.

> *"I love them that love me; and those that seek*
> *me early shall find me."* Proverbs 8:17

As I pray, I believe into that love. This verse also tells us that those who seek Him, find Him. In earnest desire, I turn toward the Lord as I believe into these words, that God is a God who loves me and who I can know. I can find His thoughts; I can know His will and His direction in my life.

> *"And the LORD shall guide thee continually."*
> Isaiah 58:11

Divine guidance is not just a one-time request of the Lord, where I decide to ask and He answers. It is a continual lifestyle, where, as I am yielding myself to the Lord, I am coming to know Him and His ways. It becomes easier and easier for me to recognize the nudges of the Holy Spirit, first in my daily life, then in bigger decisions.

I remember years ago, because of the neighborhood, the bank I went to kept their doors locked. When I approached, they would unlock one door so I could go into the entry. Then they would unlock a second door, letting me into the bank.

I would then slide my deposit through a tiny slot, just big enough for the money to fit through, to the teller sitting behind bullet proof glass. Then they would let me out, one door at a time, the same way they let me in.

One particular day, I decided I really did not want to go to that bank; I would much rather enjoy a pleasant ride while I listened to some nice worship music and drove to a bank some distance away that did not lock their doors and gave lollipops to their customers.

It was a beautiful, sunny day, and I was anticipating taking that ride. But as I was preparing to go, I felt the check of the Holy Spirit. That check caused me to understand I was to go to my own bank, the one I always went to closer to my home. I did not understand why, but I obeyed.

Later that day, I heard on the news that there was a random shooting at a stoplight on the very road where I would have been driving, right about the same time I would have been driving by, had I gone to the bank that gave lollipops. The Lord spoke to me in that moment, "There is no safer place to be than in the center of God's will."

This understanding has brought me great peace in many situations since, as I have remembered the Lord's words to me. I am so glad I sensed and heeded that check of the Holy Spirit.

Obedience comes from a lifestyle of becoming sensitive to the Lord and His presence, through time spent with Him, and the practice of obeying Him. I have learned as much from the times I did not obey, as from the times I did. Both ways, I was hearing! Knowing that, platforms of faith were built where, next time, I was quicker to trust.

I remember a time I was in Ghana and the Lord told me to go sit under a particular tree at a particular time. I obeyed, and exactly what the Lord showed me would happen, happened, and so much more!

A door of ministry opened, and I was able to go village to village, sharing in many churches. How thankful I was that I had gone and sat under the tree as the Lord had directed me! There are relationships I treasure today that came from that one act of obedience.

Scripture tells us we are not to be as a mule, who has to be dragged in the right direction.

"Be ye not as the horse, or as the mule, which have no understanding: whose mouth must be held in with bit and bridle, lest they come near unto thee." Psalm 32:9

Instead, we are to become so yielded to the Lord, that He can guide us with His eye.

"I will instruct thee and teach thee in the way which thou shalt go: I will guide thee with mine eye." Psalm 32:8

Have you ever had a relationship like that with someone? There has come such a level of intimacy that you can tell just by looking at their eyes what they want, what they are thinking, how they feel.

This is the level of relationship that the Lord desires us to have with Him, where that inner knowing of the

Lord begins to govern our lives, guiding us in the choices we make.

Very clearly, scripture is a primary way the Lord leads us, giving us instruction, wisdom, and direction through His Word.

"Thy word is a lamp unto my feet, and a light unto my path." Psalm 119:105

The peace of God is to govern our lives. There may be pros and cons and some unsettled feelings during a time of transition, yet there is an underlying peace which surpasses all understanding that we learn to recognize as we walk with the Lord.

"Thou wilt keep him in perfect peace, whose mind is stayed on thee: because he trusteth in thee." Isaiah 26:3

"For you shall go out with joy, and be led forth with peace." Isaiah 55:12

"And let the peace of God rule in your hearts." Colossians 3:15

"And the peace of God, which passes all understanding, shall keep your hearts and minds through Christ Jesus." Philippians 4:7

The fact that we encounter trouble does not mean we are in the Lord's will or not in the Lord's will, for in this world we will have problems.

"These things I have spoken unto you, that in me ye might have peace. In the world ye shall have tribulation: but be of good cheer; I have overcome the world." John 16:33

While not everything is good that happens in our lives, there comes a working of God for good through it all, for those who love Him.

"And we know that all things work together for good to them that love God, to them who are the called according to his purpose." Romans 8:28

That "good" is the formation of Christ in us. Trouble becomes a servant when we learn to respond rightly in the Lord's hands.

"For whom he did foreknow, he also did predestinate to be conformed to the image of his Son, that he might be the firstborn among many brethren." Romans 8:29

Scripture makes it clear that integrity is to guide the decisions we make.

"The integrity of the upright shall guide them." Proverbs 11:3

In good times, in hard times, the Lord has promised to guide His people continually. It is not just in difficult situations, but also in those things we think we understand, that we need His direction. Notice the word "all" in the following verse:

"Trust in the LORD with all thine heart; and lean not unto thine own understanding. In all thy ways acknowledge him, and he shall direct thy paths." Proverbs 3:5-6

I remember a dream Hattie Hammond had once. In her dream, someone brought her a complicated piece of music. As she looked at the complexity of it, she cried out, "Oh God, help me!" She put her fingers to the keys, and a beautiful melody came.

Then they brought an easy piece of music, one she was very familiar with. "I can do that," she thought to herself. As she confidently started to play, the discord was so bad it woke her up! The Lord showed her it was not just in the complicated things, but also in the simple, that she needed His help.

We may not always understand everything that happens. We may not always know how things are going to end up! But we can understand that God loves us. He has a divine plan for our lives! He is all-knowing and all-powerful. He is present; He is not just the God of yesterday or of tomorrow; He is the God of today. And He is a rewarder of those who seek Him.

As we walk in integrity, as we apply His Word in our lives, as we acknowledge our dependence and our need to hear from Him, there is a rest we come into, knowing that as we stand in simple faith today, tomorrow is also in His hands.

The important thing is that we are standing in faith and trust now, in the place God has us today. As we do this day by day, we grow into a poise of spirit that will continue to trust the Lord, whenever and however He moves in our lives, no matter how big or small our situations might be.

"Abba, Father!" These words may be, at times, the only words we have. But they are a powerful prayer, one that positions us to rely on our heavenly Father. This cry enables us to pray not words limited by our own thoughts, opinions, or understanding, but rather into the greatness of who God is, and His plan for us.

As the psalmist prayed, may we too maintain this posture:

> *"Cause me to hear thy lovingkindness in the morning; for in thee do I trust: cause me to know the way wherein I should walk; for I lift up my soul unto thee."* Psalm 143:8

But the Lord Said

"You have opened my ears and given me the capacity to hear [and obey Your word]." Psalm 40:6 AMP

Loren Cunningham, founder of YWAM, wrote a book titled, *Is That Really You, God?* This is a question we all can relate to at one point or another in life.

In fact, through the years, from time to time I have left that book sitting on a table where I can see the title, as an expression of my own heart to the Lord. Loren said that as a young child, through the godly example of his mother, he came to understand that the Lord will give guidance when we seek Him for it.

Years ago, my dad was at a crossroads. He was getting much advice as he consulted and prayed with various people. Time went on until, finally, one day I asked him what he was going to do. He told me he still did not know.

I was aware that certain thoughts shared with him had been excellent, so I asked him why he did not follow some of the advice he had already received. I will always remember his reply: "Because so far all I have heard is a lot of opinions. I am waiting for a word from the Lord."

Unless we have developed a sensitivity for *"inner hearing,"* we may miss the leading and direction of the Lord at a very critical time. Our ability to choose by reason has its place, and there are times when it may be acceptable for us to weigh the pros and cons concerning a decision as to direction and purpose for our lives.

But it is extremely important that we have also developed our "spiritual capacity" to hear, for there are times when the Lord desires to lead us up into a higher level than our natural reasoning alone can take us.

There is an example in the Old Testament of how this higher level of "spiritual hearing" changed the course of history. After Saul had failed through disobedience, then lack of repentance, the Lord sent Samuel to the house of Jesse to anoint one of Jesse's sons to be the next king of Israel.

When Samuel arrived, Jesse called seven of his sons to stand before Samuel. As Samuel stood looking at Jesse's sons, based on the guidance he had received from the Lord, it would have been natural for him to assume that one of the sons standing before him was the one the Lord had chosen.

As Samuel looked at Eliab, tall and handsome, he appeared to be the perfect king. "Surely," Samuel thought, "this must be the Lord's anointed."

> *"But the LORD said unto Samuel, Look not on his countenance, or on the height of his stature; because I have refused him: for the LORD seeth not as man seeth; for man looketh on the outward appearance, but the LORD looketh on the heart."* 1 Samuel 16:7

"But the Lord said..." Thankfully Samuel heard! As Samuel continued to look at Jesse's other sons, he said to Jesse, *"Are here all thy children?"* And Jesse replied,

"There remaineth yet the youngest, and, behold, he keepeth the sheep." Samuel said, *"Send and fetch him: for we will not sit down till he come hither."*

When David, the youngest, arrived, the Lord told Samuel, *"Arise, anoint him: for this is he. Then Samuel took the horn of oil, and anointed him in the midst of his brethren: and the Spirit of the LORD came upon David from that day forward"* (1 Samuel 16:11-13).

What if Samuel had not been sensitive to the guidance of the Lord and Eliab had been chosen as king instead of David? What did the Lord see when He looked at Eliab's heart, that Samuel did not see when he looked at his outwardly pleasant appearance? We can find the answer in the following situation, which the Lord foreknew.

All the armies of Israel were in a state of fear and trembling as Goliath challenged and mocked them. All but David.

David was full of faith from worshipping and singing to the Lord through the long nights that he faithfully tended his father's sheep. While alone with God, he had overcome difficulties and built platforms of faith in his life, upon which he could now stand. Because of this, he was ready and willing to go and face Goliath.

Eliab, however, not only lacked faith and courage himself to go out to meet Goliath, but he also mocked David, the vessel whom the Lord was about to use to bring Israel into victory. Angered by David's faith, Eliab tried to discourage him by saying, *"I know thy pride, and the naughtiness of thine heart."*

In essence, Eliab goaded David, "Who do you think you are? The only thing you are capable of is watching a few little sheep. Go back and take care of them!" (1 Samuel 17:28).

Scripture tells us that David turned away from Eliab (1 Samuel 17:30). Rather than reacting, we need to know when to turn away and move on with those things God has placed in our hearts!

When the Lord sent Samuel to Jesse's house to anoint a king, He foresaw the battles Israel would face. As Samuel's natural rationale began to conclude that Eliab was the one, the Lord told Samuel no.

Because He knew Eliab's heart, Eliab was not the one He was choosing to lead His people. Fortunately, Samuel had a spiritual ear to hear, and he was able to move beyond his own logic, into obedience with the Lord's desire.

We tend to look at things through our natural eyes and reason things with our minds. We can make charts, list all the pros and cons, and arrive at very logical and seemingly good decisions, but we may still miss God if we have not come into this higher level of spiritual hearing.

> *"For my thoughts are not your thoughts, neither are your ways my ways, saith the LORD. For as the heavens are higher than the earth, so are my ways higher than your ways, and my thoughts than your thoughts."*
> Isaiah 55:8-9

At this present time, there is an urgent need for those who can hear and see as the Lord hears and sees. It is very important that we know the thought and intention of the Lord concerning that which is taking place in the world today, aside from all natural appearances, logic, and popular opinion. To come up into this level of spiritual hearing, we must become sensitive to the Lord's thoughts and heart, and responsive to the guidance of the Holy Spirit.

This level of spiritual sensitivity develops as we spend quality time in His presence. We must become inwardly quiet, that we might discern His thoughts and His heart, so we can know how to rightly respond to the things we hear, and also pray according to His will.

> "But the natural man receiveth not the things of the Spirit of God: for they are foolishness unto him: neither can he know them, because they are spiritually discerned." 1 Corinthians 2:14

Spiritual things are spiritually discerned. If I desire to understand spiritual things, I must become spiritually sensitive. Apart from the Holy Spirit, there is no way to understand spiritual things. I must be willing to set apart time for my natural mind to become quiet from my own thoughts and come into submission to His Lordship.

In recognition of my utter dependence on the Lord, I must value and prioritize this level of spiritual hearing. I must be absolutely convinced of the necessity of receiving understanding from the Holy Spirit, then make room for that in my life activities. This is the only way I can perceive, or understand, spiritual things.

> *"Now we have received ... the Spirit which is of God; that we might know the things that are freely given to us of God."* 1 Corinthians 2:12

True spiritual understanding is birthed by the Holy Spirit. As we commune with the Lord in an attitude of worship, becoming inwardly quiet and sensitive to our Lord's presence, our hearts open up to receive those things that He has prepared for those who love Him.

> *"But as it is written, Eye hath not seen, nor ear heard, neither have entered into the heart of*

man, the things which God hath prepared for them that love him." 1 Corinthians 2:9

"But the LORD said..." We need to know, as never before, what the Lord is saying at this present time, not only concerning our own lives, but also that which He desires to do in the world today through the body of Christ. May we be a part!

"Who hath ears to hear, let him hear." Matthew 13:9

Watching at His Gates

"Blessed is the man that heareth me, watching daily at my gates." Proverbs 8:34

Recently I met someone for a cup of coffee. As I drove up, they were standing on the sidewalk looking in the direction I would be coming. What a nice feeling to see them standing there watching for me! As I pulled in, they walked up to my car ready to greet me. I knew I was welcome!

How much more it pleases the heart of God when we set ourselves to watch for Him. Proverbs 8:34-35 speaks of not only a blessing, but the favor of God on those who watch at His gates, waiting at the posts of His doors.

"Blessed is the man that heareth me, watching daily at my gates, waiting at the posts of my doors. For whoso findeth me findeth life, and shall obtain favour of the LORD."

In Isaiah we see that the posts of the doors moved at the voice of them that cried "holy," then the house was filled with smoke, or the manifest presence of God.

> *"And one cried unto another, and said, Holy, holy, holy, is the LORD of hosts: the whole earth is full of his glory. And the posts of the door moved at the voice of him that cried, and the house was filled with smoke."* Isaiah 6:3-4

In that glory there came a further working of the Lord in Isaiah's life which involved both repentance and impartation, enabling him to become joined with the purpose of the Lord.

We are living in a time of visitation. There is nothing we can do of ourselves to cause it to happen, but as we watch and wait at the posts of His doors, we please the heart of God.

> *"I love them that love me; and those that seek me early shall find me."* Proverbs 8:17

The Lord will not leave those who are watching for Him standing there alone on the sidewalk! He will come and make Himself known.

> *"That I may cause those that love me to inherit substance; and I will fill their treasures."* Proverbs 8:21

There is an urgency of spirit to seek a greater release of the Lord's presence and the moving of His Holy Spirit in greater ways. As we spend time waiting at His gates in worship and prayer, may we watch in expectation for His coming, that we might spend time with Him. Two earnest, heartfelt prayers I often pray are quite simple: "We love You, Lord!" and "Come, Lord Jesus, come."

May His presence ever increase in our lives as we seek Him, that like Isaiah experienced, we too might experience a further catching up into His purposes today. The Lord is looking to see if any are watching for His coming. He will come where He is wanted!

Urgency of Spirit

"And the posts of the door moved at the voice of him that cried, and the house was filled with smoke." Isaiah 6:4

Some time ago, a friend mentioned an "urgency of spirit" in pursuing God's glory. As I proceeded with my duties, suddenly I realized I was singing in a way I had not experienced in some time. Later, I recognized it was the releasing of God's presence that caused me to worship with such abandonment. I remembered experiencing this before, many years prior, in a powerful way, and I realized it was that same dimension of God's presence again being released.

For months after that, I continued to experience what I called "a quiet visitation," marked by the presence of the Lord. In some past moves of God, people were encouraged to spend time soaking in the presence of the Lord. He is again releasing His presence in places where the door is open for Him to come in, that He might further fill us as He works within our hearts.

I continued to think about what this "urgency of spirit" might mean. There were words I had carried in my heart for years, about a visitation yet to come, the releasing of God's glory, pure and holy from the throne of God. I believe we are living in that timeframe now and will experience the presence of the Lord in even greater ways.

But what did it mean to have an "urgency of spirit?" I thought of my friend who had shared those words; I had sometimes jokingly called them the moseying prophet. They obviously heard from the Lord and had a depth of spiritual understanding, but how could someone so laid-back speak of such an urgency?

When I understood, I was amazed. It had to do with knowing something was at hand, feeling an urgency to "get ready," but doing nothing in our flesh to try to make it happen. As I thought about this, I thought of two contrasting examples in scripture.

Sarah knew she was going to have a child. Rather than focusing on "getting ready," because of the "urgency" she felt, she tried to make it happen through her own efforts instead of waiting on God's timing. God's intention was not aborted; that joy still came, but Sarah sure went through a lot of grief.

By way of contrast, there was also an "urgency of spirit" that caused Naomi to leave Moab, and Ruth to follow her. Ruth too was going to have a son, but because neither Naomi or she knew it, their flesh did not get in the way.

Naomi did recognize God was working as His plan began to unfold. Naomi told Ruth to "sit still" until they saw how the matter would fall (Ruth 3:18). God's intention was fulfilled unhindered. How they rejoiced!

This "urgency of spirit" is very real today. Much is happening in the world and in our own nation. We are on the threshold of an end time move of God such as we have not seen. The culmination of the ages is about to burst forth as the glory of the Lord is revealed and covers the earth.

May our flesh not react to the "urgency" we may feel, but may we position ourselves in Christ as we prepare our hearts, watching at His gates, waiting at His doors, so as God moves, we hear and respond rightly.

If you remember the parable in Matthew 25, all ten virgins had lamps. Lamps speak of salvation, a free gift. Yet only five had bought oil. Oil speaks of the anointing, that which comes from time spent with the Lord. There is cost involved, choices we make. May our lamps be full, that when the door opens and the Lord comes in greater ways, we might be "ready" to enter into what God is doing.

I remember my dad saying that the five wise *and* the five foolish are in us — the deciding vote is ours! Are we going to be wise, or foolish?

May we be wise in the choices we make today. May we be prepared, poised and ready, with oil in our lamps.

Staying Under the Cloud

"At the commandment of the LORD the children of Israel journeyed, and at the commandment of the LORD they pitched: as long as the cloud abode upon the tabernacle they rested in their tents." Numbers 9:18

While facing various situations, I have been keenly aware of some basic principles which may encourage you as they have me. Let me say it like this:

The first chapter of Genesis is so much more than the glorious account of creation. It is about God Himself!

God is mentioned thirty-two times in just this one chapter. It begins with the words, *"in the beginning God."* Then *"the spirit of God moved."* Then again and again, *"God said"* creative, powerful, authoritative words. It is all about God!

God has always been faithful to meet me in every situation. Yet there have been times when I have done things of my own accord. God has at times blessed it or has even blessed through bringing a correction. But it was something I was doing and asking Him to bless, hoping He would.

How different it is when something *begins* at His initiative, or if we have prayed and then waited for a word from Him! How much more confidence we can have as we walk it out, knowing this began in God, thus as we simply continue to follow Him, we will come to His intended end.

In Numbers 9, we see the children of Israel were trained by commandment to be sensitive and responsive to the presence of God. To move when He moved. To wait when He waited. It did not matter if it was a long time or a short time — they were to stay under the cloud of His presence.

I have often prayed into this verse: *"But without faith it is impossible to please him: for he that cometh to God must believe that he is, and that he is a rewarder of them that diligently seek him"* (Hebrews 11:6).

Faith is the substance, or that which undergirds what we hope for, until it comes into material manifestation. Waiting is often involved, during which time our faith pleases the Lord.

Yet when decisions come or there are choices to make, do we wait for God? Do we really believe that "God is?" That He is present and active in our lives? That He speaks and moves? That He rewards those who seek after Him?

Or do we at times think nothing will ever happen unless we get out there and make it happen ourselves?

The Lord told Walter Beuttler once, "You go, you pay. If I send you, I'll pay." How often have we gotten ourselves into situations of our own making, rather than waiting for God's initiative, guidance, and provision?

How patient God is as we are willing to enroll, then learn in the school of His Spirit. The Lord is raising up a people today who are sensitive and responsive to His presence. How important it is that we come into this level of guidance, not only for our own safety, but that there might be fruitfulness in the things we do.

May we come into a place of listening faith, sensing His moving and hearing His voice, then staying in step with Him, not lagging behind or running ahead. May we enter into that place of His *rest* as we learn to wait and then follow His divine initiative.

> *"Come unto me, all ye that labour and are heavy laden, and I will give you rest."* Matthew 11:28

There is a place of oneness with Himself that the Lord is calling us up into. It is a place of His approbation, of intimacy of relationship with Him.

> *"Come, my beloved, let us go forth into the field ... there will I give thee my loves."* Song of Solomon 7:11-12

Notice both verses start with the word "come." That is the key! I can think of no greater thing to have today, than the favor of God resting on our lives.

As we learn to stay under the cloud of His presence, may we move when He moves and wait when He waits.

"At the commandment of the LORD they rested in the tents, and at the commandment of the LORD they journeyed." Numbers 9:23

How I love the cryptic picture found in Ezekiel 1, of that happening corporately. This type of corporate function is also what caused the walls of Jericho to fall (Joshua 6:10, 20). We will see victories of that magnitude and greater today, as we learn to follow the leading of the Holy Spirit, first individually, then corporately.

From a place of listening faith, individually, and corporately, may we learn to abide in oneness with the Lord, as we experientially come to know His moving and speaking.

May we see Him in our circumstances and come into alignment with His purposes. May the Lord bless us with a deeper revelation of Himself, His ways, and an understanding of His workings in our lives.

Together, may our eyes stay on Him!

Section 3
Relationships

Beautiful Feet

"How beautiful are the feet of those who bring good news!" Romans 10:15 NIV

Feet can be anything but beautiful, showing their years of faithful service. Yet the Word says our feet are beautiful when we bring the good news of the gospel to others.

There is so much bad news out there today. How wonderful that we can turn our thoughts to good news – the fact that God loves us; He has a plan and purpose; He will never leave us or forsake us; He is all-powerful; He sits on the throne; His purposes will be fulfilled!

Some tend to focus on the traumas of life rather than on the good things. Yet the Bible tells us:

"Finally, brethren, whatsoever things are true, whatsoever things are honest, whatsoever things are just, whatsoever things are pure, whatsoever things are lovely, whatsoever things are of good report; if there be any virtue, and if there be any praise, think on these things." Philippians 4:8

The Amplified Bible expresses it like this:

"Finally, believers, whatever is true, whatever is honorable and worthy of respect, whatever is right and confirmed by God's word, whatever is pure and wholesome, whatever is lovely and brings peace, whatever is admirable and of good repute; if there is any excellence, if there is anything worthy of praise, think continually

*on these things [center your mind on them,
and implant them in your heart]."*

In any weather, I can open the door of my multi-function office/utility room just enough to see outside. Today as I write, I see the different colors of green in the trees. I can see flowering dogwoods, a beautiful blue sky with fluffy clouds, and dandelions growing in the grass. How colorful they are! How much beauty there is if we will but look for it!

It is our choice to see the glass half empty or half full. It's not that we don't care, engage in, or pray about things going on politically and socially. God cares about all these things, and we are joined with Him in His caring.

But He is the head; we are the body. He's God; we're not! As we come before His throne in faith, believing for His ultimate purpose to be fulfilled, may we also find joy, as He does, in the good things that are around us.

The scriptures say we are the salt of the earth (Matthew 5:13). Salt adds flavor to food, making it more tasty; it also has preserving qualities.

When the Lord looks at the earth, He does not just see all that grieves Him. He also sees that "salt" which He takes pleasure in: our lives and our worship. As He sees faith in the earth, it pleases Him. He is pleased with those who are putting their trust in Him, submitting to His inner working, becoming one with Him, that He might find expression through them.

May we too, find that which we can take pleasure in, and focus on that, giving thanks to the Lord, for He is good! He is all-powerful and all-knowing. He sits on the throne! His purposes will be fulfilled. If you look at the end of the Book, He wins! He is victorious and triumphant! And so are His people!

How beautiful are your feet as you bring the good news of the gospel to others, not only believing in your own heart, but taking the time to encourage someone else. May the Lord lead you to someone you can speak a word of life to! May that light shining in you touch others for His glory. May God bless you today ... and bless others through you!

Crinkled Eyes

"A man that hath friends must shew himself friendly." Proverbs 18:24

One day as I was grocery shopping, a lady stepped in front of me. I smiled to smooth the situation, then, all of a sudden, I realized I had my face mask on, and she couldn't see my smile. I exclaimed, "Oh, you can't see I'm smiling!" She replied, "I can see you're smiling by the crinkle in your eye!" And we both crinkled our eyes.

The song, "Hallelujah to the Lamb," by Don Moen, helps express what is in my heart today. This song speaks of standing in the midst of a multitude from every tribe, tongue, people, and land; all of us, as God's people, "redeemed by the blood of the Lamb," giving thanks to the Lord for what He has done in our lives.

In this song, a commitment is made that with all our strength, we will continue to give thanks and praise to the Lord all our days. Then the song becomes a prayer, asking the Lord to release His power to work in us and through us, making us more Christ-like, so that others will see His glory and worship Him too.

Some years ago, I was in a place where men and women of all ages, from different places in the United States and different countries around the world, from the depths of their hearts and with all their strength, were singing this song over and over. It was powerful as the presence of the Lord bore witness to the oneness being expressed in the room.

How the Lord loves us and delights in our coming together in Him! This is the Lord's desire for mankind. Yet we live in a fallen world where not everyone is living by Christ's standards. We see hate and injustice, often heart-breaking. How are we to respond?

One of the most powerful warfares we will ever win is when we act contrary to a prevailing spirit. My role model for this has always been Corrie ten Boom. During World War II she did not give in to the hate all around her in the concentration camps, but continued to believe in God's Word and pray for others, even praying for those who were persecuting her.

As I learned of what she endured, yet how she maintained her own heart and, as a result, had an impact even in the midst of suffering, it has always challenged me. The day came when Corrie was released from the cruel oppression of the prison guards. She then went around the world speaking about God's love.

We see this same example in Jesus on the cross. He committed His own spirit to His heavenly Father as He prayed for the very ones who nailed Him to the cross.

What He endured never changed who He was or marred His spirit. In spotless perfection, He paid the price for our sin, that we might have new life in Him; that together, every nation, tongue, tribe, and people, might become one in Christ Jesus.

During one of our daily Bible reading times, my husband, Allen, read from the Epistles of John, first in one translation, then in another. To highlight a few of the scriptures:

"But if we walk in the light, as he is in the light, we have fellowship one with another, and the blood of Jesus Christ his Son cleanses us from all sin." 1 John 1:7

"He that says he is in the light, and hates his brother, is in darkness even until now." 1 John 2:9

"In this the children of God are manifest, and the children of the devil: whosoever does not righteousness is not of God, neither he that loves not his brother." 1 John 3:10

"He that loves his brother abides in the light, and there is no occasion of stumbling in him." 1 John 2:10

"Beloved, let us love one another: for love is of God; and every one that loves is born of God, and knows God." 1 John 4:7

As I write this, I again think of my encounter in the grocery store. Perhaps we had different backgrounds or even different colors of skin. We both wore facemasks. Yet we both had "smiling eyes." When I smiled and she smiled back, rather than conflict, peace and goodwill were generated, which brightened my day, and I believe it did hers too.

May we "crinkle our eyes" every time opportunity comes! Even as Corrie ten Boom's life shone through the darkness, may something different be seen in us in those times when someone "cuts in front of us." May we always be part of the solution, a witness that will draw others to Christ. May others find peace and forgiveness in Christ as He is seen and glorified through our lives.

> *"And they sung a new song, saying, You are worthy to take the book, and to open the seals thereof: for you were slain, and have redeemed us to God by your blood out of every kindred, and tongue, and people, and nation."* Revelation 5:9

The world did not give us this new song! Nor can the world take it away! It is who we are in Christ Jesus. His love binds us together. May His love be seen through us in the earth today. We are being made ready to be joined together for all eternity.

We have a new song! Let this be our testimony!

> *"And he has put a new song in my mouth, even praise to our God: many shall see it, and fear, and shall trust in the LORD."* Psalm 40:3

Together, let us worship the Lord with our lives and with all our hearts. He is worthy to be praised! May many come to know the Lord, His peace, His presence, and His love, because of what they see in us, the redeemed of the Lord. May our lives speak! Stand for truth!

We are one in Christ Jesus because of what He did for us on the cross.

> *"O sing unto the LORD a new song: sing unto the LORD, all the earth."* Psalm 96:1

> *"Go ahead — sing your new song to the Lord! Let everyone in every language sing him a new song."* Psalm 96:1 TPT

Love One for Another

"This do, and thou shalt live." Luke 10:28

The Lord said to the church in Sardis:

> *"And unto the angel of the church in Sardis write ... I know thy works, that thou hast a name that thou livest, and art dead. Be watchful, and strengthen the things which remain, that are ready to die."* Revelation 3:1-2a

The believers in Sardis had a reputation (name) that they lived. Perhaps they rightly believed, but they did not have a *personal experience* with the One in whom they believed. Jesus most certainly was alive, but they were dead.

Yet there was hope for them, as there is for us, no matter what our present spiritual experience may be. It is only when we are satisfied with and remain in our present state of "death" that we miss the "more" God has for us.

It is not enough to have a "name" because we have the right doctrine and stand for the truth. The believers in Sardis did this, yet they remained spiritually dead. The Lord requires us to "act" upon that which we know.

Thus, the open door was set before the church in Philadelphia:

> *"And to the angel of the church in Philadelphia write ... I have set before thee an open door, and no man can shut it: for thou hast a little strength, and hast kept my word, and hast not denied my name."* Revelation 3:7-8

The church in Philadelphia speaks of "phileo" love, which is a "love that responds to love." Their genuine, practical (being practiced) love for one another resulted in this "open door" that had been set before them, which no man could close.

When a lawyer asked Jesus what he was to do to inherit eternal life, Jesus asked him what was written in the Law.

> *"And he answering said, Thou shalt love the Lord thy God with all thy heart, and with all thy soul, and with all thy strength, and with all thy mind; and thy neighbor as thyself."*
> Luke 10:27

Then Jesus said, *"This do, and thou shalt live"* (Luke 10:28).

In order to have a vital relationship with the Lord, we must have right actions toward others. The Lord loves people so much that what we do for others will be the same as if we had done it unto the Lord Himself.

We can better understand this considering how carefully we speak to a parent about their child. They take it very personally, because they delight in their child. So it is with our heavenly Father. We are His handiwork, fashioned in His likeness. As He continues to work in our lives, the Lord takes it very personally how we treat one another.

"Come, ye blessed of my Father, inherit the kingdom prepared for you from the foundation of the world: For I was an hungred, and ye gave me meat: I was thirsty, and ye gave me drink: I was a stranger, and ye took me in: Naked, and ye clothed me: I was sick, and ye visited me: I was in prison, and ye came unto me." Matthew 25:34-36

Then the righteous asked, *"When did we do these things?"*

"And the King shall answer and say unto them, Verily I say unto you, Inasmuch as ye have done it unto one of the least of these my brethren, ye have done it unto me." Matthew 25:40

These scriptures were opened to me one day when, after ministering in a service, I was looking forward to getting alone and playing my autoharp for the Lord. Someone who did not feel well was spending the night at our house. Even so, I was desirous of my time alone with the Lord, and I was determined not to lose it.

As I sat down to play, much to my surprise, the Lord showed me that I was to go in and play for my guest. Later, I understood. As I ministered to "them," I was ministering to "Him."

The Lord has called us to "be" a witness (Acts 1:8). This "witness" is more than just speaking the Gospel to another. Our attitudes and actions, not just our words, share the life of God's Word with others.

The Lord told the church in Philadelphia that He, who had the key of David, had given them an open door. What He opened, no man could shut; what He shut, no man could open (Revelation 3:7).

This speaks of an authority which is given only through oneness with the Lord. Because they had an experiential love relationship with Him and with each other, the Lord set this open door before them. They were encouraged to enter through, into a deeper place of cooperative relationship with the Lord.

The church in Philadelphia was distinguished from those in the church in Sardis who had the right *doctrine*, but they did not have the right *experience*. Therefore, the Lord had said they were "dead." They were content to pride themselves in their religious beliefs, rather than seeking the outworking of those beliefs in their daily lives.

> *"And hereby we do know that we know him, if we keep his commandments ... whoso keepeth his word, in him verily is the love of God perfected: hereby know we that we are in him."* 1 John 2:3-5

Little choices make a big difference in who we become. Once when about to park in a garage, another car approached "my" space at the same time I did.

I could have pressed my way into this space, but I determined I would give, and not allow a hardness to come into my heart. I motioned to the other car to take the space. Was I amazed when they went right on by! I might have hardened my heart for no reason!

"My little children, let us not love in word, neither in tongue; but in deed and in truth." 1 John 3:18

We may not realize that each time we make a decision, we are being either hardened, or we are developing a sensitivity of spirit toward the Lord. As we strive to know His commandments and keep them, there is an inner transformation that begins to take place. Finally, we become as living stones, members of the church that our Lord so desires; not a church in name only, but one with an open door.

"We know that we have passed from death unto life, because we love the brethren. He that loveth not his brother abideth in death." 1 John 3:14

Paul said, *"I count all things but loss for the excellency of the knowledge of Christ Jesus my Lord: for whom I have suffered the loss of all things, and do count them but dung, that I may win Christ ... being made conformable unto his death; If by any means I might attain unto the resurrection of the dead"* (Philippians 3:8, 10-11).

Literally, I have found that, in time, difficulties do become "as nothing" in light of the inner working of God in my life. As I determine to maintain mercy, truth, and love, my heart stays soft toward the Lord, enabling Him to change me as He also lifts me into His higher purposes.

Paul speaks of this priority in his life, and of his desire for inner transformation. Then he continues, *"if by any means I might attain unto the resurrection of the dead."* Paul is not expressing concern about his salvation here. The Greek translation helps us understand that Paul is desiring an "out-resurrection from among the *living* dead."

Paul added, *"I press toward the mark for the prize of the high calling of God in Christ Jesus. Let us therefore, as many as be perfect, be thus minded"* (Philippians 3:14-15).

Paul was seeking to go beyond his present experience. May we, too, always stay open and desirous of all God has for us, as the Lord draws us into an ever-closer relationship with Himself, that we might be lifted up into a fuller participation with Him in that which He is doing today.

There is always hope for "more" if we will not settle just for doctrine, but pursue the outworking of those truths in our daily lives.

Love Perfected in Me

"If we love one another, God dwelleth in us, and his love is perfected in us." 1 John 4:12

"Love" is a fruit of the Spirit, an "attribute," or spiritual quality, that is developed within our lives. This *"fruit of the Spirit,"* love, will be formed within me through the choices I make as I walk in the way the Lord has ordained for me to walk.

Our willingness to love will be tested! I choose to love. I choose to forgive. These choices are doors which enable the "workman" of my life to work within me in the formation of my new nature. God is the "workman." I am the product.

"For we are his workmanship, created in Christ Jesus unto good works, which God hath before ordained that we should walk in them." Ephesians 2:10

Notice the word "should" in the above verse. As I submit my life to the Lord, God is working in me to will and to do His good pleasure. As I choose to walk on the paths that God has before ordained for my life, His divine favor, or approbation rests on me. The Lord continues to draw me to Himself in a love relationship, as He continues to also work inside me, making me more like Him.

God is love. Love is not something that God chooses to do as a duty, rather, it is His very nature to love. I have been predestined to be "conformed" into the image and likeness of God. As He is, so are we to be in this world. We are called to be partakers of His divine nature (1 John 4:17; 2 Peter 1:4).

This quality of divine love must grow on every level and in every aspect of my life. Choices are to be made actively. I am to contend for love. I am to contend for forgiveness. I am not to let things settle in my heart, things that would weigh me down and choke me. I must desire, then choose, to love and forgive.

As I make these choices, the "fruit of the Spirit" is formed within me. My nature changes. Soon, it is no longer just a choice to love, but it becomes my reaction, the way I respond, no matter the circumstance. Why? Something (self-centered self) has died within me through the choices I have been making. Now, it is no longer the Adamic, but Christ's nature living in me (Galatians 2:20).

This is the level of spirituality that the Lord desires to work within our hearts, that there can come forth this change deep within us. John talks about God's love being "perfected" in us, as we keep His Word, love one another, and dwell in love.

> "But whoso keepeth his word, in him verily is the love of God perfected: hereby know we that we are in him." 1 John 2:5

> "No man hath seen God at any time. If we love one another, God dwelleth in us, and his love is perfected in us." 1 John 4:12

> "Herein is our love made perfect, that we may have boldness in the day of judgement:

because as he is, so are we in this world." 1
John 4:17

As we love, there is no occasion of stumbling in us.
Love will help keep us from falling, from error, and
from sin.

> *"He that loveth his brother abideth in the*
> *light, and there is none occasion of stumbling*
> *in him."* 1 John 2:10

If we love, we have passed from death into life. In
other words, we have passed from mere religious
form, from outward show and ceremony, into an up-
resurrection from among the living dead, into a life of
communion and fellowship with the Lord.

> *"We know that we have passed from death*
> *unto life, because we love the brethren. He*
> *that loveth not his brother abideth in death."*
> 1 John 3:14

In scripture, we are commanded to love God and
others.

"Thou shalt love the Lord thy God with all thy heart, and with all thy soul, and with all thy strength, and with all thy mind; and thy neighbour as thyself." Luke 10:27

"Love worketh no ill to his neighbour: therefore love is the fulfilling of the law." Romans 13:10

To love, and also to forgive, often requires humility.

"He hath shewed thee, O man, what is good; and what doth the LORD require of thee, but to do justly, and to love mercy, and to walk humbly with thy God?" Micah 6:8

This takes something beyond our own life: *His* love abiding inside us. As we spend time in personal communion with the Lord, may we receive of His Spirit and life, that His Word and love might become a greater personal reality in our lives.

"And hope maketh not ashamed: because the love of God is shed abroad in our hearts

by the Holy Ghost which is given unto us."
Romans 5:5

Again, we can pray into these verses and other scripture verses, as we open our hearts for the Lord to touch us through them. For me, it usually is not just one prayer, but prayer over the course of time.

As the Lord answers, working deep within our hearts, we will begin to recognize His working and the opportunities we have to make choices in our life circumstances. What joy as we begin to notice the difference in ourselves! It becomes no longer I, my old nature, but now *His* nature being seen in me!

This inner change is our testimony and His delight! The Lord is looking for a harvest that resembles His Son, the firstborn of many brethren (Romans 8:29). May we be part of those who the Lord can take pleasure in! (Isaiah 53:11).

Lord, I desire to be as You are...

Dwelling in Love

"If ye keep my commandments, ye shall abide in my love; even as I have kept my Father's commandments, and abide in his love." John 15:10

The Lord defines loving Him as not just *saying* we love Him, but by *living* as if we love Him. If we love Him, we will be faithful to keep His words. As we keep His words, we abide in Him, and He abides in us. In that abiding, we abide in His love.

If ever there was a time we needed to guard our attitudes and maintain that place of abiding in His love, it is now! Offense seems to be everywhere. How important we keep our spirits clear, that the Lord might use us as light in the turbulence and darkness all around.

Key to maintaining a right attitude are the personal decisions we all must make: Am I looking for the good or the bad? Am I going to love or hate? Am I going to criticize or stand in the gap and pray? Am I going to abide in Him and dwell in love, that He might use me? Or give in to lesser feelings?

When difficult things happen, offenses often come as well. We must then make a choice. Are we going to carry offense? Or choose to forgive? Are we going to love and trust the Lord, by abiding (living) in His words, that He might abide in us? Then use us as a door for Him to enter into situations? Are we willing to believe God for a turning, in which He works everything together for good?

There are troubles in this life, that's for sure (John 16:33). Yet as Christ becomes the focus of my love and the center of my life, He promises to work that which is not so good, for good (Romans 8:28). Sometimes as I'm praying, I envision a pancake turner, like you would use to flip eggs. Then, I pray for a Holy Ghost pancake turner to flip what is happening and work it together for His glory!

As our supreme example, when Jesus was on the cross, He prayed, *"Father, forgive them, for they know not what they do."* He then, in love, commended Himself into the hands of His heavenly Father (Luke 23:34; Luke 23:46). When we, too, take this posture, the total victory of the cross is made manifest in our lives.

According to 1 John 2:5, a way to know we are in Him, is if we are loving.

> *"But whoso keepeth his word, in him verily is the love of God perfected: hereby know we that we are in him."* 1 John 2:5

In John 15, Jesus teaches that the key to abiding in Him is love, or our heart attitude toward one another. Through choices, I learn to dwell in His love; first because of my love toward the Lord, and then in the outworking of His love toward others. Though it starts as my choice, He works in my life until it is no longer just a choice, but now my new nature to love.

The Lord is bringing us up into a new place of love, so that if we see a fault or a weak area in another, we will choose to stand in prayer and intercession for them, rather than criticizing, until that area begins to develop.

Francis Frangipane said in his book, *Truth, Holiness, and the Presence of God*, "Anyone can pass judgment, but can they save? Can they lay down their lives in love, intercession, and faith, for the one judged?

Can they target an area of need, and then, rather than criticizing, fast and pray, asking God to supply the very virtue they feel is lacking? And then, can they persevere in love-motivated prayer until that fallen area blooms in godliness? Such is the life that Christ commands we follow!"

Needs all around us are giving opportunity for His nature and character to be worked inside us. God is love. He is bringing forth a people who resemble Him.

Are we willing to dwell in love? To love each other? Are we willing to care about each other? We will never become holy by criticizing other people. We will never be brought nearer to God through finding fault.

Are we willing to move beyond our own personal reactions and yield to the Lord so He can use us in the midst of difficult circumstances?

We cast the deciding vote. Are we going to become bitter or better? The difference is in the "I."

May the Lord renew our minds and empower us to live righteous lives today. May we have a right perception of things. May we guard our spirit concerning attitudes and choices that would hinder the quality of our spiritual life. May we center our lives in Christ Jesus, that we might find His heart and His thoughts and give expression to Him as faithful and effectual witnesses in the earth today.

> *"For I know whom I have believed, and am persuaded that he is able to keep that which I have committed unto him against that day."*
> 2 Timothy 1:12c

> *"Being confident of this very thing, that he which hath begun a good work in you will perform it until the day of Jesus Christ."*
> Philippians 1:6

The Lord is raising up a righteous people for His end time glory in the earth today. A people born from above, who dwell in His love, that His love might be manifested in and through their lives. May we be a part of that people!

Treasuring Our Relationships

"Christ in you, the hope of glory!" Colossians 1:27

"Behold, how good and how pleasant it is for brethren to dwell together in unity!" Psalm 133:1

Whether we are writing or speaking, "Christ in you, the hope of glory" is at the core of

our message as we pray and believe to be a part of that people God is preparing for His end time purposes.

Paul spoke of his strong prayer and desire that Christ be formed in the Church.

"My little children, of whom I travail in birth again until Christ be formed in you." Galatians 4:19

While we can often think of the words "Christ in you" as applying to us individually, there is a corporate "you" to whom they also apply. Christ is coming back to be admired in his saints (2 Thessalonians 1:10).

Many years ago, Ivan Q. Spencer spoke of "the reproduction of the Christ within His many-membered body." He spoke of the forming of Christ within us, and of the Lord drawing a body of overcomers into a place of intimacy with Himself. When I heard his words, they resonated in me, and I have kept them close over the years.

These thoughts have been stirring in me again, as I'm experiencing a deeper understanding of the reproduction of Christ in a "many-membered body." Christ in us, the hope of glory! Joined together under His headship, in right relationship with God, and with each other.

How the Lord longs for this coming together of the body of Christ. An overcoming people in whom Christ has been formed, through whom He can work and move. Revelation 5:9 and other verses speak of a great multitude who come together in unity of heart from every nation, tongue, tribe, and people. What a glorious calling! What a glorious people to be part of!

Recently, my husband Allen taught on conflict resolution and building friendship in marriage. These skills can be applied to other relationships as well. As I listened, I realized afresh how important our relationships are. What a big part they play in God's purpose being fulfilled in and through our lives, individually and corporately!

We can desire, determine, and learn to walk in right relationship with one another, starting in the home, then flowing out to the body of Christ and into the community. Psalm 133:1-3 speaks of the anointing that flows down where good relationship (unity) is:

"Behold, how good and how pleasant it is for brethren to dwell together in unity! It is like the precious ointment upon the head, that ran down upon the beard, even Aaron's beard: that went down to the skirts of his garments;

As the dew of Hermon, and as the dew that descended upon the mountains of Zion: for there the LORD commanded the blessing, even life for evermore."

Joined together, we can become a people in whom Christ can be seen and glorified, that there might be a fuller manifestation of His presence among us. Our lives are enriched as we learn to love and walk in right relationship with others.

My prayer is that the understanding of "Christ being formed within" will burn in other hearts, as it does in mine. I have been blessed to see some people so transformed by the Christ within, that His heart and nature finds expression in them, come what may. Their lives challenge me to continue to yield to the Lord and His inner working in my own life.

May we all press toward that high calling of God. As we allow the Lord to work within, may we also be open to learning some new skills! May our relationships be strengthened. May Christ be seen in and through our lives, singularly and together, in the way we treat one another – at home, in the church, in the workplace, and in the community.

As we open the door for the Lord to work within us, may we become His habitation, a resting place for the presence of the Lord. Christ in *you*, the hope of glory. Christ in *us*, a yet greater hope of glory, that there might be an even greater manifestation of His glory, presence, and power in the communities, countries, and places God has us.

Christ in you. Christ in me. Christ in us! How important our relationships are! May we treasure them, as God-given gifts.

Section 4

Forgiveness

Do Not Be Swallowed by a Whale!
A Willingness to Forgive

"You are a gracious God, and merciful, slow to anger, and of great kindness." Jonah 4:2

I have been humming a song that I sang as a child. "*I don't want to be a Jonah and be swallowed by a whale. Down to Nineveh I must go if the Savior tells me so. Shout aloud you must be born again!*"

This little song pretty much sums up the book of Jonah. But what is it really saying? Simply that if the Lord calls us to go somewhere, then we must go? Yes, this is true; but there is much more in this song.

The key is found in why Jonah did not want to go to Nineveh. Was it just because they were a Gentile nation, and he was a Jew? Interestingly, Joppa is the very place where God, 800 years later, gave a vision to Peter, causing him to go to Cornelius's house, a Gentile, releasing the outpouring of the Holy Spirit on the Gentiles (Acts 10:1-29).

Or was it perhaps because of the great wickedness in Nineveh? The sins of Nineveh were great (Jonah 1:2; Nahum 3:1-4). Were they so evil that Jonah did not want to go? Might it be that Jonah was afraid? These people were known for their brutality; no one wanted to become captive to their cruelty.

Why didn't Jonah want to go to Nineveh? As you look at Jonah's own words, the real reason is found.

> *"And he prayed unto the LORD, and said, I pray thee, O LORD, was not this my saying, when I was yet in my country? Therefore I fled before unto Tarshish: for I knew that thou art a*

gracious God, and merciful, slow to anger, and of great kindness, and repentest thee of the evil." Jonah 4:2

In other words, Jonah knew God is gracious and that if they repented, He would forgive them. And he did not want these people forgiven! Why? Nineveh was the capital of Assyria, an enemy to Israel. To hear judgment was coming on Nineveh in forty days was good news for Israel; it put them in a much better position. It must have been a joy to Jonah's ears!

But if Jonah warned them as God was asking him to do, they might repent. And if they repented, God might forgive them. Nineveh might be spared, and Israel's position would not be strengthened. Jonah did not want to see that happen, so he decided not to go. He personally preferred to see Nineveh judged.

Though initially Jonah resisted the call to Nineveh, after God dealt with him, he obeyed. Nineveh believed and repented, just as Jonah was afraid they might; thus, God's judgment was withheld. This made Jonah very angry. The book ends with the Lord rebuking Jonah for his anger.

Has there ever been a situation in your life where you really did not want to see God forgive someone? You would rather see the judgment of God on them? Where when someone got blessed, you were disappointed rather than happy?

I don't want to be a Jonah and be swallowed by a whale. No matter how terrible we may see a crime or an individual to be, the Lord would give them opportunity to repent.

I think of Corrie ten Boom forgiving the very guard who brought so much suffering to her and caused her sister's death. God forgave the guard because he repented. Corrie had to be willing to forgive too. When she did, the love of God flooded her heart.

Notice the mercy of God, both toward Nineveh, a sinful people, and toward Jonah, a disobedient servant. The Lord's judgment on both wickedness and disobedience is very clear. Yet prior to judgment is warning, with an opportunity to repent. Both Nineveh and Jonah received an opportunity to repent.

The same grace that Nineveh received after they repented from their evilness was the same grace that Jonah needed, when he finally repented for his disobedience. May we always be thankful God is merciful, that He forgives all those who repent. In the same way He forgives others, He forgives us.

Because Jonah did not want to do what God was asking him to do, he tried to flee from the presence of the Lord. Psalm 139:7 asks, *"Whither shall I go from thy spirit? or wither shall I flee from thy presence?"*

In the verses that follow, Psalm 139:8-12, we see there is nowhere we can go that God is not there. Paul adds to this in Romans 8:38-39 as he assures us there is nothing that can separate us from God's love.

As we come to truly understand that God is always there, may assurance fill our hearts. He hears us when we call! His mercy endures forever! Great is His faithfulness (Isaiah 65:24; Psalm 106:1; Lamentations 3:23).

Because God is omnipresent, it was impossible for Jonah to flee from the presence of the Lord. Jonah went in the other direction. A storm came, and he was cast overboard. But when Jonah prayed out of the fish's belly, God was still there. The goodness of God brought Jonah to repentance and gave him another opportunity to go to Nineveh.

Jonah took advantage of his "second chance" and went, though he complained to God. How much better when we take things to God in prayer, rather than complain to people. God in His faithfulness answered Jonah again as He addressed Jonah's wrong attitude, then showed Jonah His heart instead.

The book of Jonah was written not only so that we can learn from Jonah's mistakes, but as a further revelation of the very nature and character of God. He is a loving, compassionate, ever-present God, who takes no delight in judgement. His desire is that all would come to repentance, that none would perish.

> *"I have no pleasure in the death of the wicked; but that the wicked turn from his way and live."* Ezekiel 33:11

> *"Whosoever shall call on the name of the Lord shall be saved."* Acts 2:21

"If we confess our sins, he is faithful and just to forgive us our sins, and to cleanse us from all unrighteousness." 1 John 1:9

The story of Jonah also gives us a picture of what the Lord is looking for in us. If the Lord desires to bring repentance to someone, we must be willing to move in cooperation with Him as He brings it about. We too, must be willing to forgive even as God is willing to forgive those who repent. Likewise, we must also forgive ourselves.

May our hearts be like God's heart, full of compassion and mercy, delighting in repentance, willing to forgive.

A favorite verse of mine has been hanging on my wall for years:

"He has showed you, O man, what is good; and what does the LORD require of you, but to do justly, and to love mercy, and to walk humbly with your God?" Micah 6:8

May this be engraved in our hearts, evidenced by our attitudes and actions.

The Power of Forgiveness

"Forgive, and ye shall be forgiven."
Luke 6:37c

Forgiveness is a choice. When we forgive, we have made a conscious decision to do so. Yet true forgiveness will go beyond that decision, to an actual change in our feelings. We can and should make the decision to forgive; that is our part, our responsibility in obedience to God's Word. But only the Lord can truly change the deep, inner feelings of our hearts. And He will, as we are willing.

A role model for me has always been Corrie ten Boom, who suffered as a prisoner in a Nazi concentration camp. Corrie not only endured the cruelty of the prison guards herself, but she also witnessed the painful death of her beloved sister under their brutality.

After Corrie's release from prison camp, she traveled to many places, ministering to others the love of God from her own experience of forgiveness. Then one night after Corrie had finished speaking, she was surprised to see one of the cruelest of the prison guards walking up the aisle toward her.

Painful memories came as the former guard approached her and then told Corrie that he had repented and knew God had forgiven him, but that it would mean a lot to him if he could hear her say that she too forgave him. Corrie thought she had been living in total forgiveness, yet her heart froze as she remembered her sister's suffering.

As Corrie stood there, she knew she had to do this. She had noticed that among those who had been in the concentration camps, those able to forgive were the ones able to live normal lives. Furthermore, the Lord commanded her to forgive. Yet her body became like wood, and she could hardly move.

Corrie determined to say three simple words, "I forgive you." With effort, she reached out her hand to shake his, when all of a sudden, the Holy Spirit flooded her. She began to cry "I forgive you, I forgive you," as she embraced the man. Corrie made the choice; God changed her heart.

> *"And hope maketh not ashamed; because the love of God is shed abroad in our hearts by the Holy Ghost which is given unto us."*
> Romans 5:5

I remember a situation, years ago, that was very difficult for me. Even so, I felt I had come too far in the Lord to let unforgiveness grow within. I understood that nothing can hinder a life more than a root of bitterness, which in time would entangle and darken a person's spirit. So, I was determined not to allow unforgiveness to settle inside me.

For months, I kept choosing to forgive, releasing those involved. Yet inside, I still felt negative emotions. I kept refusing those feelings and choosing to forgive, only to have the feelings come back, and I would have to choose again.

Then, one day, the Lord intervened in my life. I was overwhelmed as the Lord manifested His presence and I saw the excellency of who God was, and then the wonderfulness of what He was doing in my life. In that "light," this hurtful situation flashed again before my mind — except this time, by way of contrast it became as nothing in the "glory" of His presence. That offense was literally cremated inside me, never to trouble me again.

Later, the Lord manifested His presence again, this time for hours, revealing His love. He loves those who love Him above all else, and those who seek Him shall indeed find Him.

> "I love them that love me; and those that seek me early shall find me. That I may cause those that love me to inherit substance; and I will fill their treasures." Proverbs 8:17, 21

The forgiveness that we receive and are to extend to others, is exemplified in the New Testament, in the book of Philemon. A servant had taken some of his master's property and run away. Later, this servant came into contact with Paul and became a believer. Realizing the necessity of making the situation right,

Paul sent this servant back to his master with a note asking that he be forgiven of his wrongdoing.

In this example, aspects of divine forgiveness are paralleled in the forgiveness that Paul sought for this man. The servant had been unprofitable to his master, and there was offense. Yet Paul was beseeching for his forgiveness.

Paul not only made intercession for him, but offered to make a substitute payment for the debt the man owed. Paul asked that this man not only be restored, but elevated to a new relationship; that he be received not just as a servant, but also as a brother. What a beautiful picture of what Christ has done for us!

Paul did not justify what this man did, but he pointed out that perhaps it was for this purpose, that he might find salvation. Romans 8:28 does not tell us that all things are good. Rather, it promises *"that all things work together for good to them that love God, to them who are the called according to His purpose."*

On days when things seem to be going wrong, I pray, "Lord, turn these things for good." We all face problems in this life. Yet all things do work together for good if we will but take time to look to the Lord. This gives us hope in any situation.

The master could have refused to forgive his runaway servant, but Paul reminded him that he also owed his own redemption to Paul's ministry. As we walk through life and realize how gracious the Lord has been to us, there comes a humility that makes it easier for us to forgive others. Where would any of us be if only perfection could please the Lord? We should never demand perfection of others, when we ourselves need grace.

> *"And be ye kind one to another, tenderhearted, forgiving one another, even as God for Christ's sake hath forgiven you."*
> Ephesians 4:32

Being able to walk in the deeper truths of the Spirit ultimately becomes easy when we realize that the very heart of the gospel is simply to love God with all our hearts, and our brother as ourselves. In this, we pass from death to life — an out-resurrection from mere religion into a life of fellowship with the Lord. This is the key to an overcoming life!

> "We know that we have passed from death unto life, because we love the brethren." 1 John 3:14a

Even as faith without works is dead, so the profession of love without forgiveness is dead. May our love for the Lord always be evident in our lives. Personally knowing God's love motivated Corrie ten Boom to make the choice to forgive; the Lord responded by manifesting His love through her.

May each of us fight the good fight of faith and forgiveness. When things come my way, I always remind myself, if Corrie could forgive that prison guard, there is no one that I cannot forgive.

The choice is ours to make.

The Importance of Clear Vision

"I have shewed thee new things from this time, even hidden things, and thou didst not know them. Thus saith the LORD, thy Redeemer, the Holy One of Israel; I am the LORD thy God which teacheth thee to profit, which leadeth thee by the way that thou shouldest go." Isaiah 48:6b, 17

Riding through the mountains of Pennsylvania, I leaned forward, intently trying to see the road. I knew I was going in the right direction, but I lacked immediate vision. My windshield wiper was going back and forth faithfully, doing its very best to help. But it just was not working anymore, the way it had in the past.

Finally, I pulled over on a somewhat familiar road, feeling quite certain I could find the help I needed there. Sure enough, there was an auto parts store, right by my favorite coffee shop, too! Within minutes,

I was back on the road with a new set of windshield wipers, a nice hot drink, and a clear view of where I was going.

I could have struggled and struggled, and even made it to my destination the way things were. But with just a little much needed change, I was able to enjoy my ride and make the trip with a lot less effort.

As I listened to my music, I sang along with the song I had been playing over and over, time and time again, "How Great Is Our God!" The singers put forth a passionate call, "Sing with me, how great is our God," and my heart worshipped along with them. The presence of God flooded my car as I now drove with ease. I was on the road that I knew I was to be on, and now I also had the clarity of vision to stay on it.

Clarity of vision. How important it is that we not only sense the direction the Lord desires to take us, but that we also have the clearness of vision to follow the road He would lead us on, step by step.

So many things try to cloud our view, smudging up the windshields of our lives. However, the Lord has promised us His Holy Spirit to lead and guide us, that we might avoid the ditches of this life and stay on the path He has ordained for us.

There are times when disappointments, hardships, or other hurtful situations come our way, threatening to blur our view. As we allow the Holy Spirit to wash these away, while He also is working deep within us, our vision stays clear, so we can continue to move forward on the path before us.

Sometimes the old just does not work anymore. It is time for a change! We need a fresh word from the Lord, a fresh touch of His Spirit in our lives.

Maybe we need to stop and get some advice or ministry from a friend. Maybe we need to make room for that new thing the Lord would add to our lives. Or maybe we just need to make more time for physical rest or to spend time in our own personal prayer closets.

One thing is certain: The Lord who has called us, will also direct us if we will but believe and ask. We are to move by faith in the direction we know the Lord is leading us, yet we are to stay flexible to the continued leading of His Holy Spirit.

A prayer at the foundation of this level of divine guidance is found in the Psalms.

> *"Cause me to hear thy lovingkindness in the morning; for in thee do I trust: cause me to know the way wherein I should walk; for I lift up my soul unto thee."* Psalm 143:8

The word "cause" is very strong. It speaks of the divine activity of God, beyond my own ability or understanding, working in my life. Through God's grace we receive His enabling power, the divine strength we need day by day.

Isaiah 58 speaks of a lifestyle: humble, free from the strife of the tongue, with a heart that cares for others, which the Lord says He delights in and will bless. The Lord promises He will guide us, not occasionally, or if we get in a real jam, but continually, if we live this way.

"Then shall thy light break forth as the morning ... And the LORD shall guide thee continually ... and thou shalt be like a watered garden, and like a spring of water, whose waters fail not." Isaiah 58:8a, 11

Within the Church, there is an intimacy of relationship that the Lord is calling us up into. The Lord does not want to have to drag us around like stubborn mules. His desire is for us to come into that place where our hearts are so turned toward Him that we can sense the gentle nudges of His Holy Spirit within, as we yield and learn to move with Him.

"I will instruct thee and teach thee in the way which thou shalt go:

I will guide thee with mine eye." Psalm 32:8

As I focus on the greatness of God and come into a place of worship that is based simply on who He is, there is a presence of God that is released into my life. In that intimacy of relationship, as I learn to live in fellowship with Him, the Lord will direct me not just in former ways, but new ways, for it is a new day that we are entering, and there are new things the Lord wants to do in new ways.

"Behold, I will do a new thing; now it shall spring forth; shall ye not know it? I will even make a way in the wilderness, and rivers in the desert." Isaiah 43:19

There are times when we can be very determined just to make the old work. It is like that faithful windshield wiper that had served me for so long. The time came when it simply could no longer meet the need at hand. A change had to take place. I had to be willing to take the time to pull over, then, to pay the price for the new.

David prayed in the Psalms:

"Teach me to do thy will; for thou art my God: thy spirit is good; lead me into the land of uprightness." Psalm 143:10

What a confession: Thou art my God! How *great* is our God! He is good! He is *The* Lord God, the Almighty One; but more than that, He is the Lord *Our* God, the

Almighty One! He is faithful! He leads and guides His people!

I can pray for this level of guidance and believe for it, as I also consecrate my life to the Lord. We express our desire for God's blessing on our lives not just through the words we speak, but through the choices we make. His blessing is available to all who would value it and sincerely desire His divine activity in their lives.

My vision? Christ! His victory! His greatness! As day by day, I am learning to follow His leading in my life.

A Peace that Surpasses All Understanding

"Be careful for nothing; but in every thing by prayer and supplication with thanksgiving let your requests be made known unto God. And the peace of God, which passeth all understanding, shall keep your hearts and minds through Christ Jesus." Philippians 4:6-7 KJV

Another translation words it like this:

"Don't worry about anything; instead, pray about everything. Tell God what you need, and thank him for all he has done. Then you will experience God's peace, which exceeds anything we can understand. His peace will guard your hearts and minds as you live in Christ Jesus." Philippians 4:6-7 NLT

There is a peace that surpasses all understanding, that comes not from our circumstances or what is happening all around us, but from the indwelling presence of Christ.

Our inner peace is important and is to be treasured, guarded, and maintained. It can be hard not to react when we see or hear things happening, yet how essential we set aside our own reactions and come to a place of quietness, that we might seek the heart of God instead.

In peace there is healing. From a place of peace, I can more easily find direction. In peace there is quietness and rest. In peace there is victory! As I become peaceful, I can better find my position in Christ, then stand with greater impact.

"He hath shewed thee, O man, what is good; and what doth the LORD require of thee, but to do justly, and to love mercy, and to walk humbly with thy God?" Micah 6:8 KJV

The Amplified Bible says it like this:

"He has told you, O man, what is good; And what does the LORD require of you Except to

be just, and to love [and to diligently practice] kindness (compassion), And to walk humbly with your God [setting aside any overblown sense of importance or self-righteousness]?"

For us to live this way is our own decision, contingent only on our own hearts and the Lord within. It does not say if people are kind or deserving, we are to behave this way. Who I am is not defined by what others do! I am who I am by the grace of God! And I live to please Him.

Living from an eternal perspective and seeing the working of a higher purpose, even in mundane things, makes it easier to deal with the provocations of this life and to maintain our peace.

Paul said in 2 Corinthians 4:17, *"We view our slight, short-lived troubles in the light of eternity. We see our difficulties as the substance that produces for us an eternal, weighty glory far beyond all comparison"* (TPT). We'll talk about this more in the next few chapters.

We live with a present purpose and a future hope. The choices we make to walk in peace may not seem to have much bearing on anything we perceive today, but they are forming who we are and will be, in eternity. These choices also have a present impact, perhaps more than we realize at times.

May we be carriers of God's light; carriers of His peace and presence. May we be ambassadors for healing, peace, and reconciliation. May we do what is right ourselves. May we be merciful toward others. May we walk humbly before God.

The Lord is raising up a people to be carriers of His presence, those who will reflect His light and help bring healing and love to others who are hurting. No matter what happens, may we always lift our hearts upward, that we might be prepared to reach outward, should opportunity come.

> *"The LORD has shown you what is good. He has told you what he requires of you. You must treat people fairly. You must love others faithfully. And you must be very careful to*

live the way your God wants you to." Micah 6:8 NIRV

"And the peace of God, which passeth all understanding, shall keep your hearts and minds through Christ Jesus." Philippians 4:7 KJV

As the Williams translation puts it: *"Then, through your union with Christ Jesus, the peace of God, that surpasses all human thought, will keep guard over your hearts and thoughts"* (Philippians 4:7).

Day by day, may He fill us with His peace and love as we turn our hearts upward, seeking His heart, His thoughts, and His ways. May we choose the Lord's blessing! May His blessing rest on our lives.

Section 5
Managing Our Time

Push Through or Stop?

"But they that wait upon the LORD shall renew their strength." Isaiah 40:31

The sun was setting, the night air getting cold. As we pushed to get done, we ran into a kink that just wouldn't resolve. Allen, not a quitter, said, "We are in the overcoming mode!" We chuckled then continued to wrestle.

It got darker and darker. Finally, I said, "I'm done, let's do this tomorrow." Knowing I wasn't one to quit either, Allen queried, "What are you saying?" I responded, "I am saying I think we're done for tonight!" Allen resignedly looked around and agreed, he too was done! We secured things for the night and tottered off to get some rest.

The next morning the sun was shining. Refreshed, Allen had some ideas he'd had time to ponder. As I listened to him work, whistling and singing, this time conquering the hurdles, I was so glad we had taken the time to get refreshed!

This is God's plan – times of working, times of refreshing. The next night we did have to push through due to inclement weather. But there are times we can stop, get refreshed, then continue. Wisdom, if we're going to make it for the long haul, is to know the

difference! When to stop, and when to go!

We see many examples of this in scripture. For instance, in Exodus 19:3 and 14, Moses went up to spend time in God's presence, then came down to minister to the people. In the life of Christ, we see the same pattern. Matthew 17:1, 9, and 14 tells us Jesus went up into a mountain apart to pray, then came down to minister to the people. Luke 9:2 and 10 shows us that Jesus trained His disciples in the same way to minister, then to take time apart to be refreshed.

I think of my dad and so many others who ran their race before us. I remember them, then I think of all the years behind me, and I thank the Lord for His faithfulness. Then I look with expectation at the years yet ahead!

May we live our lives with gusto! May we find our pattern of ministry, rest, and refreshing so we too can run, not just as in a sprint, but a marathon, making it to the finish line with joy, in the strength of the Lord!

We are living in a turbulent time, yet the Lord continues to raise up a people to be carriers of His presence, carriers of His glory. May each of us be found faithful in the place God has us!

> *"And let us not be weary in well doing: for in due season we shall reap, if we faint not."* Galatians 6:9

"But ye, brethren, be not weary in well doing." 2 Thessalonians 3:13

"Come unto me, all ye that labour and are heavy laden, and I will give you rest." Matthew 11:28

"But they that wait upon the LORD shall renew their strength; they shall mount up with wings as eagles; they shall run, and not be weary; and they shall walk, and not faint." Isaiah 40:31

May we find and sustain consistent times of refreshing, that with vigor we might complete our full course.

Running on Empty

"And they heard the voice of the LORD God walking in the garden in the cool of the day."
Genesis 3:8

Have you ever been traveling in your car while listening to some soft music and enjoying the beautiful scenery, or deep in your own thoughts, when suddenly you realized you were running on empty?

If you were fortunate enough to be in my dad's car, it tells how many miles can be driven with the remaining gas. Hopefully, there will be a gas station within range! But if you were in my car, there is only a little yellow light that blinks, leaving you guessing as to how far you can go.

The realization of emptiness, when it comes, releases a desperation. We may not have stopped to fill up before, feeling we did not have the time, or, because the price was too high. But now time and price matters little, as the urgent need to be refueled becomes a priority.

Regardless of the vehicle, there is one thing we all understand. Without proper fuel, we may be able to coast awhile, but we will not get very far. Therefore, we watch the gauge and look for places to purchase fuel. Most importantly, we avoid getting near empty.

In our Christian walk, the fuel we need is the power of the Holy Spirit. There are those at this present time who are recognizing their need. Hungry for more of the Lord, they are searching for places to "*fuel up.*"

There is an increased reawakening of a deep, inner, personal need for more of the Lord being rekindled in hearts today. Without a refueling of the Holy Spirit, we may be able to coast a little longer, but we will move little from the place we are presently at, as the energy that is needed to climb hills and face mountains is not present. Some are becoming aware that a fresh refueling is urgently needed.

Historically, there has always been a remnant that realized this need and pressed through to receive a fresh infilling of the Holy Spirit. Many, however, remain satisfied

to coast on the energy of a past visitation.

Thus, the cycle continues. There are those who have experienced a visitation. Then, the next generation may hear about it or even try to continue in all they gained. But that next generation is seldom as powerful as the first, unless they too have an encounter with the Lord. A dynamic that was present in the first is missing by only maintaining.

Today, there are those with a dissatisfied satisfaction who are crying out for more. They appreciate all the Lord has done and treasure it. Yet they sense God is still moving. They desire to be carriers of all God releases, not just past, but present, and future.

Matthew 13:52 speaks of a householder *"bringing forth out of his treasure things old and new."* I am thankful for the past. Yet for years, I have prayed that I would not park or settle as one who hears then simply maintains what they have received. Life has to grow!

I am determined that I will press in day by day for a fresh encounter with the Lord, as I embrace treasures both old and new. I desire to be among those who are joined to the Lord as the voice of the Lord continues to walk in the cool of our day (Genesis 3:8).

Looking backwards, there was a tremendous deposit in my dad's life as well as in others' lives, through John W. Follette. Some have very faithfully "maintained" the life work of John W. Follette by duplicating his tapes and writings, then guarding them. While all of that is good, my dad took those same truths, then allowed the Lord to expand them through his own life experience.

I remember very distinctly one particular Saturday night while I was the pastor of a small church in the DC area. We helped to host a monthly conference at which my dad spoke. I was making tape after tape to fill the orders, so they would be available the next morning.

While doing this, I went into a dialogue with the Lord, saying "Lord, I would gladly make these tapes for You forever if these alone would fill the need." But I could see the voice of the Lord walking in the cool of the day. I knew that as good as all of this was, it was but a foundation for that which the Lord would yet say and do tomorrow. These tapes alone could never fully meet tomorrow's need.

That which is being birthed today must be embraced and received. From that, there will always be maintainers. But there must also be a remnant that will press forward into tomorrow's truth. All that the Lord does is always progressive. When we "park," we miss.

While making those tapes many years ago, there was within me a heart's cry that I would always walk onward with the Lord, day by day; that those truths which I had already received would become a part of me, and that I might also be a partaker of the progressive revelation that is yet being revealed.

We cannot park, nor can we coast. We need to fuel up, as we are facing things today that were not an issue twenty years ago. As time moves forward there will be even more things in which we will need the wisdom, strength, and power of His Spirit to come through victoriously.

> *"Jesus said, "I am the vine, you are the branches: He that abides in me, and I in him, the same brings forth much fruit: for without me you can do nothing."* John 15:5

Without Jesus becoming a personal reality within us, we can do nothing. Today is the day we have to empty ourselves of all pride and ambition and acknowledge our need to the Lord. We have learned so much that our heads are full. But knowing cannot replace our seeking and experiencing the continued infilling of the Holy Spirit – the very presence of God Himself in our midst.

A twelve-year-old boy who had an encounter with the Lord recently was quoted as saying Jesus told him that He did not come to start a religion, but that He might have a personal relationship with each one of us.

The Lord is calling us to draw near to Him. We want Him to touch us, but He desires so much more than this. He is calling us to draw near to Him, that He might draw near to us. We are called to be a *"habitation for God through the Spirit."* A simple truth, yet how easily we can miss it. The Lord is calling us back to this one simple truth.

It is essential that we make time to get before the Lord, to seek Him with all our heart. It is time to dig trenches, to remove the rubble, clutter, yes even of religion, to get ready for fresh rain. Fresh drops of rain are beginning to fall. Even more rain will come, but it is those who are ready who will receive.

Spiritual transformation begins at salvation. We are to continue to grow in our relationship with the Lord, in which we become more Christ-like. The zeal of the Lord for His people is powerful. Isaiah 62 tells us He will not rest, nor are we to rest, until we come forth as a Holy people unto His name.

*"For Zion's sake will I not hold my peace, and
for Jerusalem's sake I will not rest, until the*

righteousness thereof go forth as brightness, and the salvation thereof as a lamp that burns." Isaiah 62:1

"I have set watchmen upon thy walls, O Jerusalem, which shall never hold their peace day nor night: you that make mention of the LORD, keep not silence, And give him no rest, till he establish, and till he make Jerusalem a praise in the earth." Isaiah 62:6-7

"And they shall call them, The holy people, The redeemed of the LORD: and you shall be called, Sought out, A city not forsaken." Isaiah 62:12

Are you recognizing that there is need in your own life? An emptiness? Do you hunger for more of the Lord's presence? Or perhaps you want to desire the Lord, but many other things keep pushing in. Try fasting one meal. As the desire for food arises, ask the Lord to take this desire and turn it into a spiritual appetite for more of the Lord.

He will fill you, if you will but stop to fuel up.

Preparation for Visitation
Keys to A Deeper Walk with the Lord

"O come, let us worship and bow down: let us kneel before the LORD our maker." Psalm 95:6

The Lord is releasing an end time anointing for those who are willing to take the time to receive it. As we spend time in His presence, learning to become quiet and to open our hearts before the Lord, our spirit will become more receptive, allowing the Lord to release His presence and anointing within us. This impartation will take place to the degree we have prepared our hearts to receive and carry the Lord's presence in our lives.

There are many marvelous benefits to setting apart quality time to spend in the Lord's presence. Our times of "waiting upon the Lord" help to prepare our hearts to receive from Him. The receptivity of our spirit is enlarged, and our spirit becomes more sensitive to His Spirit, as we spend time quietly before Him. The sensitivity of our spirit relates directly to our being able to receive, as well as being able to "walk in the Spirit." Yet, how much time do we spend each day, waiting in His presence?

"But one thing is needful." Luke 10:42a

A number of years ago, I looked at the lives of some who I felt carried an evident spiritual quality and anointing, to see how they received it. I found that each had one thing in common; they spent much time waiting upon the Lord.

Waiting upon the Lord is a time of worshipful quietness before the Lord in which we become receptive to the Spirit of God. It is not a time to make our requests known or to become passive; it is a time of expectation, in which we actively wait to be filled with His presence and fellowship with Him.

"One thing have I desired of the LORD, that
will I seek after; that I may dwell in the house
of the LORD all the days of my life, to behold

the beauty of the LORD, and to enquire in his

temple." Psalm 27:4

In our corporate gatherings, we are experiencing "touches" of visitation as we worship the Lord. As this Holy Spirit "rain" begins to fall, His presence descends, enveloping us, filling us with His Spirit. The degree to which we receive depends on the preparedness of our hearts. Quality times we have set apart to wait upon the Lord help to prepare our hearts for this fresh infilling of the Holy Spirit.

"I love them that love me; and those that seek

me early shall find me. That I may cause

those that love me to inherit substance; and

I will fill their treasures." Proverbs 8:17, 21

We should not wait upon the Lord in order to have a glorious experience in that moment. Rather, we are to become quiet and sensitive to His presence so we can begin to hear His voice. Once we begin to hear, He will lead us according to His purpose and accomplish His will in and through us. How glorious when we see this happening!

"It is sown a natural body; it is raised a spiritual body." 1 Corinthians 15:44a

As we continue to wait, there will be a progressive dying of our flesh to all the voices of our natural mind, and a subsequent birthing of the mind of Christ with His thoughts and His purpose. We should cultivate this practice of waiting upon Him in our daily life experience, until we are no longer governed or controlled by the demands of the natural realm. As we do this, we will become more sensitive, and our ear will become more and more tuned to the voice of the Lord.

"You have given me the capacity to hear and obey." Psalm 40:6b AMPC

Scripture tells us that our natural minds cannot even imagine the things that God has prepared for those who love Him and wait for Him (1 Corinthians 2:9; Isaiah 64:4). As we devote ourselves to quietly spending time in His presence, we will renew our strength and ascend into what He has prepared for us.

"Even the youths shall faint and be weary, and the young men shall utterly fall: But they that wait upon the LORD shall renew their strength; they shall mount up with wings as eagles." Isaiah 40:30-31a

In His presence, we will begin to understand the mysteries of the Kingdom. There will be a realignment of our lives. Our priorities will change from the natural to the spiritual. Our spiritual senses will be energized by His presence and restored to respond to His purposes.

"Now we have received ... the spirit which is of God; that we might know the things that are freely given to us of God." 1 Corinthians 2:12

We are being changed from one level of glory to a higher level of glory. As the presence of the Lord is increasingly made more manifest, it will create within us a hunger for more.

A mirror can reflect light into another mirror, which can be reflected into yet another mirror, as a reflection of reflected light. In the same way, we may be birthed from a certain ministry and even flow in the same anointing and echo the same teachings, but unless we personally have cultivated the presence of God by spending time waiting on the Lord, we simply will be reflecting reflected light, a dimmed reflection of the glory of the Lord.

We are to reflect the glory of the Lord in all of His brilliance. When Moses spent time in the presence of the Lord, the glory became so glorious that he was asked to cover his face. This intensity of glory resulted from his being in the presence of God for a prolonged time.

Anointed teaching can help bring us into this place, if we do not settle for the lesser and become satisfied with just hearing and repeating good teaching, without entering into the relationship from which spiritual understanding comes and is worked into our lives. Ministry should be a springboard that lifts us up into this "place by Him" where something more is being deposited into our being.

"When the day of Pentecost was fully come..." Acts 2:1

We are experiencing touches of visitation, both individually and corporately; but when the day of visitation has *fully* come, suddenly, there will come a sound from heaven "as of a rushing mighty wind," and He will fill *all* the house. This should be our expectancy as we continue to spend time in the presence of the Lord.

The receptivity of our spirit will greatly determine our ability to continue to receive as visitation continues to come and the manifest presence of God continues to increase in our midst. To the degree we have prepared our hearts to receive and carry the Lord's presence in our lives, we will receive, as we also make ourselves available for the Lord's purposes in the days ahead.

The Lord is releasing an end time anointing, if we will but take the time to receive it.

Pressing Through Busyness

"And it came to pass, that, as the people pressed upon him to hear the word of God, he stood by the lake of Gennesaret, and saw two ships standing by the lake...

And he entered into one of the ships, which was Simon's, and prayed him that he would thrust out a little from the land. And he sat down, and taught the people out of the ship. Now when he had left speaking, he said unto Simon, Launch out into the deep, and let down your nets for a draught." Luke 5:1-4

In this passage of scripture, the people were pressing upon the Lord to hear the word of God. In response, Jesus moved out a little from where they were standing, then sat down and taught them. Afterwards, He told Simon to go out even deeper.

Each of us in various ways, find ourselves pressing, or being pressed, to accomplish one purpose or another.

The most important question we could consider is, are we "pressing" toward that which has eternal value, or toward those things that will pass away? Are we being faithful in those things the Lord has called us to, or are we busy with other things?

The Apostle Paul said in Philippians 3:13-15:

> *"Brethren, I count not myself to have apprehended: but this one thing I do, forgetting those things which are behind, and reaching forth to those things which are before, I press toward the mark for the prize of the high calling of God in Christ Jesus.*
>
> *Let us therefore, as many as be perfect, be thus minded: and if in anything you be otherwise minded, God shall reveal even this to you."*

Somehow, we all become very "busy." As a result, there are many things that hinder our devotional times. We must reject these and determinedly press through them in order to have some quiet times with the Lord.

The Lord notices and responds whenever we rise above all these "things" to seek Him. In Luke 5, as the people "*pressed*" to hear Him speak, Jesus entered into one of the ships, pushed out a little from the shore, then sat down and taught them.

The "shore" relates to our everyday activities. Jesus pushed beyond the shore to teach principles relating to a deeper walk and relationship with Him. He then told Simon to *"Launch out into the deep."* The depth to which He will take us is contingent upon the desire of our heart.

As we open our hearts to the Lord and continue to press towards Him, the Lord is faithful. We may have to press through much busyness. Or we may be pressing through difficult circumstances. Regardless, the Lord sees those who are faithfully pressing towards Him out of a hunger to know Him more. These He will sit down and teach, sowing the seed of the Kingdom deep within their hearts.

In Luke 5, Jesus sat down in the boat, then taught the people who stood intently listening. Matthew chapter

13 tells us what He said. He dealt with attitudes and thoughts within their own hearts, and ours too, that would be a hindrance to the growth and development of the word of the Kingdom which was being sown deep within their hearts.

The more time we spend in the Lord's presence, the deeper the seed will go, and the stronger the roots will become to withstand the storms of life. Spiritual understanding, discernment, and submission to the ways of the Lord will develop within our spirits and then be worked out into our everyday lives.

As the Lord calls us to launch out into the deep and we respond, our natural and spiritual lives will begin to function in harmony. As we hunger after more of the Lord, a progressive working of the Lord takes place in each of our lives.

The Lord seeks to do a "new thing" in each of us. This will be seen only when the fruit of the seed that has been planted within us has been faithfully cared for, that it might develop into full maturity.

There is always more available in God. The apostle Paul said he did not feel he had apprehended everything that the Lord had for him. But he was reaching out and pressing forward, as he ran straight toward the goal to win the prize, the upward call of God that is found in Christ Jesus.

He then admonished those desiring maturity that they too should be *"thus minded."* Paul said that if we had this poise of spirit, that if in anything we were *"otherwise minded,"* the Lord would show it to us.

I have expressed this desire to the Lord, that He would show me, if in any of my actions, I am *"otherwise minded"* than what I am confessing to the Lord. And the Lord answers!

Some time ago, I noticed that I was checking my emails first thing each morning. Often there were messages resulting in a busyness that cut into the time I had set aside to be alone with the Lord. My time would be gone, and I would have to begin my day without personal communion alone with the Lord.

The Lord showed me I was saying one thing, but doing another. I said I was putting Him first. I said He was the priority of my life. It was why I had set my alarm early, to have that time alone with Him! Yet I was allowing other things to push into that time and take the time that had been set aside for Him.

How often we do this and do not even realize it! Yet if our heart is truly toward the Lord, He will surely show us if *in anything we be otherwise minded,* that our experience might match our confession.

Busyness! It will never go away. It is a part of modern-day life. But within that, we have choices we can make. As we prioritize, cutting away that which is not needful, and rightly ordering that which is, the Lord who sees our hearts will help us in all that needs to be done.

For years I had a quote by Walter Beuttler sitting on my desk. "Give the Lord priority, and He will give priority to you."

Our part is simply to be faithful in putting Him first.

He will do the rest.

Section 6
Victorious Living

Filled With Assurance

"But we have this treasure in earthen vessels." 2 Corinthians 4:7

As we were walking up our road one morning, I spontaneously started to sing:

"Blessed assurance: Jesus is mine! Oh, what a foretaste of glory divine! Heir of salvation, purchase of God, born of His Spirit, washed in His blood. This is my story, this is my song, praising my Savior all the day long; this is my story, this is my song, praising my Savior all the day long."

I was rather surprised! I hadn't heard that song lately, but it was just bubbling up inside me. Delighted, my musician husband joined in, and of course he knew all the words to all the verses, so we sang them all. What joy it brought as we walked our little dog Jethro up the street singing praises to the Lord!

We sang the same verses over and over because that was the melody that the Lord was obviously blessing! Hattie Hammond used to say, "When you strike gold, stay there." And that's just what we did!

Words from the song continued to echo in my heart all week. Blessed assurance, Jesus is mine! What a foretaste of glory divine! Born of His Spirit! Washed in His blood! Praising my Savior all day long. This *is* my story! This *is* my song! Hallelujah!!! I'm praising my Savior, all the day long!

Praises kept welling up in my heart. What a privilege, what a joy!

This assurance and joy we experience is ours because of what Jesus did for us on the cross. It is an inner joy, based on our relationship with the Lord Jesus Christ and His work inside us. It is not based on what is happening or on what we have or don't have. It comes from our fellowship with Him and His presence inside us.

> *"Although the fig tree shall not blossom, neither shall fruit be in the vines; the labour of the olive shall fail, and the fields shall yield no meat; the flock shall be cut off from the fold, and there shall be no herd in the stalls:*
>
> *Yet I will rejoice in the LORD, I will joy in the God of my salvation.*
>
> *The LORD God is my strength, and he will make my feet like hinds' feet, and he will make me to walk upon mine high places."*
> Habakkuk 3:17–19

As I found myself singing "Blessed Assurance" and reflecting on the words over and over again, I decided to research this song's history. It was written by Fanny Crosby in 1873. I read in the details of Fanny's life that a doctor improperly treated an eye infection she had as a baby, causing scars on her eyelids which blinded her for life.

Her mother, widowed just a few months later, worked as a maid, so Fanny's grandmother raised her. Fanny's grandmother taught her the Bible and the importance of prayer. When Fanny had a hard time learning and was sad, her grandmother encouraged her to pray for knowledge.

When Fanny was twelve, she had opportunity to attend a school for the blind, and she later taught there for twenty-three years. She married a former student, a popular organist in the New York area. They had one child who died shortly after birth.

It was one evening while Fanny was visiting her composer friend, Phoebe Palmer Knapp, that Phoebe got a melody for which Fanny immediately had the words. "Blessed assurance, Jesus is mine!" Together, they continued to write the beautiful lyrics that are still sung today.

"Blessed Assurance" is one of over 8,000 songs that Fanny wrote the words to, many still popular today.

What treasure she carried! Paul said in 2 Corinthians 4:7, *"But we have this treasure in earthen vessels, that the excellency of the power may be of God, and not of us."*

I am so thankful for the treasure that we, too, carry. I am thankful for the joy and love that is ours in Christ Jesus.

In the third verse of "Blessed Assurance," Fanny wrote, "Perfect submission: all is at rest, I in my Savior am happy and blest; watching and waiting, looking above, filled with His goodness, lost in His love."

Paul prayed that we too, would know the love of Christ and be filled with the fullness of God (Ephesians 3:14-19). Scripture also speaks of being filled with the Spirit; filled with fruits of righteousness; filled with the knowledge of His will; filled with joy (Ephesians 5:18; Philippians 1:11; Colossians 1:9; 2 Timothy 1:4).

This is my prayer too, that we be "full" and ever mindful of this treasure we have been so blessed with. For it is Christ *in* you, that is the hope of glory! (Colossians 1:27).

As we focus on what we do have, rather than on what we don't, may we be good stewards of what He has entrusted to us. May fruits of righteousness be seen through our lives! May we come to a place of submission and rest in Him, as the love of God and joy of the Lord fills our hearts.

Jesus is mine! And I am His! This is my story, this is my song...

Living From an Eternal Perspective

"And we know that all things work together for good to them that love God, to them who are the called, according to his purpose." Romans 8:28

In John 16:33 Jesus said, *"In the world ye shall have tribulation: but be of good cheer; I have overcome the world."* There are many problems in this life, that's for sure! Yet Jesus, the overcomer, lives inside us! We have His strength to draw on, that come what may, we too might overcome.

We can experience troubles, like a car breaking down, which are just part of this life. But there are also things some endure as a part of our Christian witness.

Paul went through tremendous hardship for the sake of the gospel:

"Of the Jews five times received I forty stripes save one. Thrice was I beaten with rods,

once was I stoned, thrice I suffered shipwreck, a night and a day I have been in the deep;

In journeyings often, in perils of waters, in perils of robbers, in perils by mine own countrymen, in perils by the heathen, in perils in the city, in perils in the wilderness, in perils in the sea, in perils among false brethren;

In weariness and painfulness, in watchings often, in hunger and thirst, in fastings often, in cold and nakedness." 2 Corinthians 11:24-27

Some who are reading this have paid a price for their faith. Others may live in places where the cost of being a Christian is increasing. In view of the hardships Paul endured for the sake of his loyalty to the gospel and zeal for the glory of God, he asserted:

"If in this life only we have hope in Christ, we are of all men most miserable." 1 Corinthians 15:19

But! Paul lived from an eternal perspective. He saw beyond the hard times, into what God was doing in the midst of the difficulties he faced, things of eternal value.

Paul saw an eternal purpose being fulfilled in those who were being touched through his life. He confidently declared that even more people would yet hear the gospel, then give thanks to the Lord, resulting in an even greater glory to God.

> *"For all things are for your sakes, that the abundant grace might through the thanksgiving of many redound to the glory of God."* 2 Corinthians 4:15

Because of his deep desire for the glory of God to be seen, Paul continued with hope and expectation, counting his present suffering as nothing in the light of eternity.

> *"For which cause we faint not; but though our outward man perish, yet the inward man is renewed day by day.*

For our light affliction, which is but for a moment, worketh for us a far more exceeding and eternal weight of glory;

While we look not at the things which are seen, but at the things which are not seen: for the things which are seen are temporal; but the things which are not seen are eternal." 2 Corinthians 4:16-18

When we face a situation that in itself is not good, be it just a part of this life and this world's systems, or perhaps a price we pay for the sake of our testimony, as we trust the Lord, He will in some way cause good to come from it. God is faithful to His Word!

We can train ourselves to look for the good. It is always there, though sometimes in hidden ways which are hard to see, or which have not yet appeared.

"And we know that all things work together for good to them that love God, to them who are the called, according to his purpose." Romans 8:28

"Be happy and glad, for a great reward is kept for you in heaven. This is how the prophets who lived before you were persecuted." Matthew 5:12 GNB

None of us would choose a difficult path, that is for sure! Yet as we come through difficult situations, if we respond rightly, not only is Christ glorified, we mature and grow as we also learn and become wiser.

May this be our burning desire: *"Christ in (us) the hope of glory!"* (Colossians 1:27). That as He is, so we may be in this life (1 John 4:17). This is the Lord's desire for each of our lives!

May our vision go beyond the things of this life, to living from an eternal perspective. For the things in this life are temporal, but God's Kingdom is eternal.

"Thy kingdom is an everlasting kingdom, and thy dominion endureth throughout all generations." Psalm 145:13

"And there is given him dominion, and glory, and a kingdom, that all people, nations, and

languages, should serve him: his dominion is an everlasting dominion, which shall not pass away, and his kingdom that which shall not be destroyed." Daniel 7:14

The Kingdom of God will be established on the earth. However, today His desire is to do an eternal work within each of our hearts.

He is the King! He rules in the land of our lives through our submission to Him. As we yield to Him, His throne is established in our hearts. Through just "one yes at a time," His government is established within us. As we submit, that which is of eternal value is taking place.

What enables us to yield to the Lord, that His higher rule might take place in our lives? Where now it is no longer our Adamic nature which is ruling, but God?

Several truths impacted my life, increasing my eternal perception, causing a desire to yield more fully to the Lord and His workings in my life. Activities otherwise mundane, became more meaningful. Hurtful situations became more fruitful. Never, as I yielded to the Lord, have I regretted it. Always, looking back, I was glad I did!

God's Word promises, *"He shall see of the travail of his soul, and shall be satisfied: by his knowledge shall my righteous servant justify many; for he shall bear their iniquities"* (Isaiah 53:11).

What a beautiful promise! It was through Hattie Hammond that I came to understand there is a Spirit-given unveiling of calvary available that we can believe for, which creates in our hearts a passion for Christ to see the fruit of His suffering and be satisfied.

After I heard this, I began praying earnestly that this passion to see Him satisfied would burn in my heart as a fire, and that all that was contrary would be burned out of me.

I also heard John Wright Follette speak of our love for Christ becoming sufficient enough to allow the cancelation of our own lives, for His. That truth touched my heart too, so I began praying for that divine displacement to take place within my life, that His life might have preeminence.

Then I reflected on Paul's words in 1 Corinthians 2:1-2, *"I came to you, came not with excellency of speech or of wisdom ... For I determined not to know any thing among you, save Jesus Christ, and him crucified."*

I prayed for that reduction in my life too, that my faith would truly rest in the power of the cross and in His resurrection life and power.

As these deep desires were imparted into my spirit, it began to change the way I saw things. My desire for the glory of God to be seen, increased. What He was doing became more predominant, and other things became less in comparison.

These "eternal perspectives" and more can be instilled in our hearts through faith and prayer. They enlarge our vision and encourage us, as we walk through life seeing in a greater way not just circumstances, but that which God is doing today.

The first time worship is mentioned in the Bible is when Abraham, who had faith in the faithfulness of

God and trust in His eternal purposes, put his all, Isaac, on the altar.

As we too worship, may the Lord build His throne within our hearts and lives. May we draw on Christ's strength as we continue on, in hope and expectation, confident of the faithfulness of God.

May that passion to see the Lord's purposes fulfilled rule in our hearts, causing everything else to fall into its rightful place.

A Triumphant Procession

"Now thanks be unto God, which always causeth us to triumph in Christ, and maketh manifest the savour of his knowledge by us in every place." 2 Corinthians 2:14

I think we would all agree, this life holds challenges! In 2 Corinthians 2:14, Paul is expressing thanks to the Lord for His enabling grace and power that *"always"* causes us to triumph in Christ, bringing a procession of victories in our lives. I love that word "always"!

My dad, Wade Taylor, used to say, "The next time the Lord lets me down will be the first!" I heard him say that many times in his eighties. But it caught me by surprise when I came across an old tape and heard him saying the same thing when he was just in his forties.

As I listened, I heard him say with a youthful voice, "I like to say the next time the Lord lets me down will be the first!" Then with a little laugh he added, "And I feel like I am going to be able to say this my whole life!" ...and he did!

I paused to think about his life – wonderful times, hard times, responsibilities he carried, things he had come through. His strong faith in the sovereignty of God, the intervention of God, and his yieldedness to the inner working of the Lord in his own life filled my mind, as a fresh appreciation for the faithfulness of God burned deep inside me.

Then I began to think of God's faithfulness in my own life. Renewed understanding flooded my heart as I knew I will be able to say the same thing right through to the end of my life too!

One translation of the Bible describes our victories as "a triumphal procession."

> *"But thanks be to God, who in Christ always leads us in triumphal procession, and through us spreads the fragrance of the knowledge of him everywhere."* 2 Corinthians 2:14 ESV

One year as I was again teaching the book of 2 Corinthians, that "triumphal procession" became highlighted to me. I saw what appeared to be a triumphant procession of people all through the ages, an endless number of people walking, each in step, as a mighty army. I marveled as I looked at the numbers, overcomers from every time in history, including today. What a privilege to join such ranks! What an awesome call!

Then I saw not only a "corporate procession" of triumph through the ages, but the "personal procession" of victories in my own life, bringing me to the place where I am now. I saw victories from past circumstances. I saw victories in the making today. Then I saw victories I didn't even know about yet, which were to become part of my life experience.

I realized as I face the circumstances of my own life, I am in step with a mighty army of those who have gone before me, those who lived victoriously in this life, and who now move in triumphant procession in eternity.

Paul gives thanks to the Lord who *always* "causes" us to triumph! That word "cause" is a strong word. It speaks of a strength beyond our own, which God *always* gives to us, as He brings us into victory.

Ezekiel 36:27 promises:

> *"And I will put my spirit within you, and cause you to walk in my statutes, and ye shall keep my judgments, and do them."*

What a glorious promise! We see this divine strength given in Acts 1:8, which tells us that *after* the Holy Ghost has come upon us, we are empowered to "be" or become a witness unto Him, everywhere we go! As believers, what strength we have within, what divine enabling power!

Through His enabling power, as we move from victory to victory, a working of the Lord takes place within our lives, changing us to be more like Him. Amazing to me, though we are yet growing in our walk and our faith, God can still use us, making Himself known to others through us.

As we face our challenges today, know there is a whole army of people who have faced their battles all through the ages, and there is a people today, rising up in faith and victory. We are called to be part of that people!

Second Corinthians 2:14 speaks of us being partners of His "endless triumph."

> *"God always makes his grace visible in Christ, who includes us as partners of his endless triumph. Through our yielded lives he spreads the fragrance of the knowledge of God everywhere we go."* TPT

Romans 8:37 speaks of us being in all things *"more than conquerors through Him that loved us."* The Passion Translation says it like this: *"Yet even in the midst of all these things, we triumph over them all, for God has made us to be more than conquerors."*

Notice the word "all." The trials we face at the moment are no exception!

We can rest assured the Lord will never leave us or forsake us (Hebrews 13:5). His grace will always be sufficient! (2 Corinthians 12:9). God is faithful, and He will always be faithful (1 Thessalonians 5:24).

May the eyes of our understanding be enlightened to know the hope of His calling and the greatness of His power toward us who believe (Ephesians 1:17-19).

With confidence we can draw on His power today and every day, whatever situation we face, for it's not our strength, but His strength made perfect in us (Zechariah 4:6; 2 Corinthians 12:9).

With grateful hearts, may we always give thanks to the Lord for His enabling power that *causes* us to triumph in Him. By His strength, may we walk in triumphant procession through the challenges we face in the world today.

As we face the ever-increasing challenging times in our day, my prayer is that we will draw on His strength and live by His power as never before, as He continues to work deep within us, changing us, using us, leading us from victory to victory, bringing a triumphant procession of victories into our lives.

In this life there will always be challenges (John 16:33). There is also a battle waging as darkness confronts light with increased ferocity. We hold fast to this promise:

> *"They will wage war against the Lamb, but the Lamb will triumph over them because he is Lord of lords and King of kings — and with him will be his called, chosen and faithful followers."* Revelation 17:14 NIV

The Fragrance of His Presence

"But thanks be to God, who in Christ always leads us in triumphal procession, and through us spreads the fragrance of the knowledge of him everywhere." 2 Corinthians 2:14 ESV

I am so thankful for the enabling power and grace of the Lord Jesus Christ that *always causes* us to triumph in Him, bringing a procession of victories in our lives! As we yield our lives to the Lord, in each of us, He is well able to perfect that which He has begun.

"Being confident of this very thing, that he which hath begun a good work in you will perform it until the day of Jesus Christ." Philippians 1:6

Though He is still working in us, there is a testimony as we continue to yield to the Lord and draw on His strength. As one translation says:

"Now He uses us to spread the knowledge of Christ everywhere, like a sweet perfume." 2 Corinthians 2:14b NLT

Acts 1:8 tells us that *after* the Holy Ghost has come upon us, we are empowered to "be" or to "become" a witness unto Him everywhere we go! What a calling! To live a life that reflects Christ, as His presence is made known to others through us.

"But ye shall receive power, after that the Holy Ghost is come upon you: and ye shall be witnesses unto me both in Jerusalem, and in all Judaea, and in Samaria, and unto the uttermost part of the earth." Acts 1:8

Notice that our primary call is to become a witness "unto *Him*." Our lives are to become as *"a Christ-like fragrance rising up to God"* (2 Corinthians 2:15 NLT).

This fragrance will be noticeable to others, becoming a witness "unto them." But first and foremost, is our witness to the Lord. Our witness to others is to be the byproduct of a life lived pleasing to the Lord.

As His presence is made known through us, some will love that fragrance that comes from our lives, and some won't like it at all.

> *"For we are the sweet fragrance of Christ [which ascends] to God, [discernible both] among those who are being saved and among those who are perishing."* 2 Corinthians 2:15 AMP

This fragrance comes through our union with Christ.

> *"But thanks be to God, for He always leads me in His triumphal train, through union with Christ, and everywhere through me keeps spreading the perfume of the knowledge of Him"* 2 Corinthians 2:14 Williams Translation

It is *"Christ in you, the hope of glory!"* (Colossians 1:27). I am a living epistle, written by the Spirit of God, read by all men. From glory to glory, I am being changed that more of Him might be seen, and less of me (2 Corinthians 3:3, 18).

John said, *"He must increase, I must decrease."* Paul professed that he died daily; that Christ lived in him (John 3:30; 1 Corinthians 15:31; Galatians 2:20).

Hattie Hammond often said, "None of us are perfect yet. If we were, God would have taken us home!"

God is not finished with us yet! He is still working in us. Paul said, *"For it is God which worketh in you both to will and to do of his good pleasure"* (Philippians 2:13).

> *"For we are his workmanship, created in Christ Jesus unto good works, which God hath before ordained that we should walk in them."* Ephesians 2:10

Notice the word "should." We don't have to! We were created with free will. But if we are wise, we will walk in His plans and purposes, that there might come a transformation in our lives. When it is not our Adamic nature, but Christ being seen in us, it is a sweet fragrance that pleases God and touches others.

There is a certain perfume I have worn for years. Its fragrance is gentle, yet I remember when I was teaching at the Bible school years ago, someone once saying, "I knew you had come this way because of the fragrance that lingered in the hall."

What kind of fragrance does our life leave when we pass by? The fragrance of His presence? Let us practice His presence, living lives that are pleasing to Him, lives where He can flow through us to touch others.

In good times ... in hard times ... and everywhere we go! May our lives be marked by the presence of the Lord. May we be as a sweet fragrance, pleasing to God as we reflect Christ, that through us, He might be made known to others.

Living Testimonies

"Fight the good fight of faith, lay hold on eternal life, whereunto thou art also called, and hast professed a good profession before many witnesses." 1 Timothy 6:12

We are living in uncertain and stressful times. How can we help? One way is by living upright lives regardless of what challenges we may face, that there might be godly examples for others to see and thus be encouraged.

A verse I have always loved speaks of Christ coming back to be admired "in" His saints (2 Thessalonians 1:10). Christ seen and admired *in* us. What a calling!

After I am saved, I am to mature and grow. My salvation is a free gift, but my character is formed through choices I make. As I yield to the Lord, He works in my life until it becomes *"yet not I but Christ"* living and being seen in me (1 Peter 2:2; Ephesians 2:8; 1 Corinthians 15:31b; Philippians 2:13; Galatians 2:20).

Song of Solomon 8:5 asks, *"who is this that comes up from the wilderness leaning on her beloved?"* There has been a change! This is our testimony! We are called to "be" or "become" witnesses unto Him, whatever the situation or circumstance, everywhere (Acts 1:8).

God gives us the enabling power to "become" that witness through the empowering of the Holy Spirit and as we learn to draw on His strength, spending quality times apart with Him in prayer, worship, and His Word. As we do, we in turn can "be" a place of refuge, strength, comfort, and encouragement to others in troubled times.

Our witness is so much more than our words. Did you ever hear the saying, "Your actions speak so loud I can't hear a word you are saying?" How important we live godly lives so our words will be credible. When what we say and what we do line up with God's Word, it's a powerful testimony.

In one of our daily devotional times, Allen pointed out that when we first heard the gospel, we looked at the life of the person presenting it, and, consciously or not, we made some decisions about the gospel, based on the life and behavior of the presenter.

He said as a child, his first Sunday School teachers were people of high moral character, with loving spiritual concern for him. Because he had high respect for them, when they taught the gospel, he believed they were speaking truth.

How I appreciate Allen's words. Not just his words, but his life, a living demonstration of what he was talking about!

Titus 2:5 directly exhorts us to good behavior so that the Word of God is not blasphemed. Satan cannot attack sound doctrine successfully, so he chooses to try to attack those who present it. Good character sustains us!

In Titus, Paul is encouraging sound doctrine, good behavior, and good works. We are to live responsible, honorable, and God-fearing lives, being self-controlled, upright, and godly; lives dedicated to God.

Do we want the gospel that we present to be accepted by those who hear? Let's heed the words Paul gave to Titus:

> *"Above all, set yourself apart as a model of a life nobly lived. With dignity, demonstrate integrity in all that you teach."* Titus 2:7 TPT

> *"Have no more to do with godlessness or the desires of this world, but to live, here and now, responsible, honourable, and God-fearing lives."* Titus 2:12 PME

I sometimes ask myself, would anyone look at my life and want to be a Christian? Would my behavior cause anyone to want to know the Lord? What do people feel when they are around me? Can they sense His presence, His peace, His love, His joy?

2 Corinthians 3:2-3 speaks of our lives as being living epistles, *"known and read of all men."* What do people see and read as they look at our lives? Our lives may be the only Bible some people will ever read. We have opportunity today, to share Christ with

others not just through our words, but through our lives.

There was an elderly lady I was blessed to have some time with, who had such a love for the Lord, something I could see and feel in her life that went way beyond her teachings or sermons, that gave me "a revelation of a relationship" that was available, causing a deep desire within me to have that same kind of relationship with the Lord. Once I saw it, and that it was available, I wanted it!

May our lives match our words! May we "be" witnesses in the time we are living in, a time when there is so much uncertainty. May our words edify, and our lives be a model of integrity. May we "be" a people in whom Christ is seen and glorified.

Section 7
The Faithfulness of God

Faith of Our Fathers – Living Still

"But continue thou in the things which thou hast learned and hast been assured of, knowing of whom thou hast learned them; And that from a child thou hast known the holy scriptures, which are able to make thee wise unto salvation through faith which is in Christ Jesus." 2 Timothy 3:14-15

One beautiful day, we could hear the sound of saws, hammers, and lawn equipment as neighbors busily made use of their "stay at home" time. It was so nice to see dads walking with children! Families sitting on porches or playing games in the yard. People of all ages, walking with someone or walking alone, but all enjoying the fresh air.

We too were enjoying being outdoors, as we had our devotional time together on the back deck. We usually had this time together in the living room; what a pleasant change of pace that day! Birds were singing, the sun was shining, it was truly a beautiful day as we listened to the hum of life all around us.

During our times of devotions together, which we have begun to call *Living Room Moments*, Allen usually reads scripture, prays, and often sings. This day was no exception, as he began to sing "Faith of Our Fathers."

As the writer so poetically put to music: despite great difficulties, the faith of our fathers stood. That same faith lives in hearts today. Because of that faith they had, and now we have too, we also will stand strong.

As Allen sang, I thought of my own dad. I remembered one day, after the Lord took him home, when I was sitting in my dad's favorite chair, praying. Clocks were ticking all around me, how my dad loved clocks!

A few weeks prior, I had started to do some work in his office; one of the first things I found was that the cable was not long enough to reach from the desk to the printer. To print, I had to take the computer over to the printer, plug it in, and then wait for it to print.

At first, I could not believe my dad never mentioned that to me! How easy it would have been for me to buy a longer cable, or rearrange the room, if only I had known!

But he was not one to complain, he liked being adaptable. I remember his smile as he would say, "I'm low maintenance!" I suppose his joy in that overrode the inconvenience; it just was not a problem to him or anything worth mentioning.

My dad and I often had a cup of coffee together. He liked to go out for breakfast, so I always tried to be free for those special times. He might be talking, or maybe I was. Or, I might be sitting there as he talked on the phone with others! Regardless, those were always times I treasured.

An incident I'll always remember happened quite a few years ago. As I was taking a walk alone, an understanding of becoming "more than a conqueror" came to me so strongly, I stopped to write it down. I drew a sketch of what I was seeing on a napkin, then wrote down my thoughts.

When I got home, I mailed the crumpled napkin to my dad. I was excited to share it with him and wanted him to see it just as I received it.

Later I heard him share the same thing, even drawing the same sketch. I was so encouraged as I listened, that I had been able to share something of value that now he was sharing too. I thanked the Lord for a spiritual ear and the understanding of spiritual truths.

It was some time after that, that I came across a teaching by my dad. To my surprise, he was speaking the same truth I had discovered, at least ten years prior to my experience! As I heard chalk squeak on the blackboard, I wondered if perhaps he was even drawing the same illustration.

I realized that I had probably heard him share on that, but I didn't remember it. Nonetheless, an impartation had gone deep into my spirit.

That deposit worked its way into my understanding in its own way, in its own time, so "personalized truth" (not just me quoting something he said, but through my own walk) might be awakened inside me and find expression. I was amazed!

My dad always prayed not just for an anointing, but that there would be an impartation of spirit and life as he spoke and prayed for others. I am so thankful for my dad and the truths that have impacted my life, and others', through his life and ministry.

The last thing we did together before the Lord took him home was to have breakfast together. I almost didn't make time. Am I ever glad I did! That too, was a conversation I will always treasure.

I learned as much (or maybe even more) from the hard times my dad went through, as from the good times. He would always submit himself to the Lord and then allow the Lord to work in his life through whatever he faced. That deep inner trust in the Lord was something I was privileged to see close up. It impacted my life beyond what I have words to say.

My dad used to say, "The next time the Lord lets me down will be the first." I too can say that, from my own experience with the Lord. How faithful our God is!

One particular truth dear to my dad's heart was his understanding of communion. Each day, he would spend extended time quietly sitting in the Lord's presence in an attitude of worship, and also take communion.

For those who knew my dad, he was tone-deaf, so he did not sing. But true worship is an attitude of the heart. In meetings, there were times when that worship deep in his heart would get stirred. As he stood at the podium, you'd hear his monotone voice saying, "Hallelujah, Hallelujah." Sometimes the Lord's presence would become so intense, waves of spontaneous, harmonious worship would break out as people responded to the presence of the Lord.

That anointing flowed from the inner workings of the Lord in his own life and from times he spent each day in the presence of the Lord. At times he would simply sit quietly in an attitude of worship, while other times, he would also read scripture, sometimes the same verse for months, as life from that verse would flow into his being. Most days he also prayerfully took communion, believing into the words Jesus said as he partook.

Communion was always precious to him. Yet I still remember when the Lord began to quicken his understanding, giving him an even greater appreciation for that which we receive when we partake of the cup and the bread, in faith.

Because of his sharing, many of us began to take communion more often. I would pray, "Lord, Your Word says if we discern Your body, we won't be sick, weak, or die prematurely. Help me, Lord. Open the eyes of my understanding to discern Your body, that I might perceive and receive of spiritual things."

Along the same lines my dad taught and believed into, Andrew Murray wrote in *The Blood of the Cross*, as he expounded on the eternal spirit of God which works in us through the precious blood of the Lord Jesus Christ. As he pointed out, everything else in life has a point of beginning and is subject to time. But that which is eternal, has no beginning and does not change.

As our faith takes hold of that which is eternal, there is an understanding that we too can pray into, that His power would be manifest in us, His power which never changes, never grows weary, and never withers, but is always fresh. My strength varies from day to day. His does not! I can draw on His strength and power!

John Hyde, better known as Praying Hyde, said when he realized that we have the power of God to draw on for all our needs (2 Timothy 1:8), he seldom felt tired, though he often prayed through the night. He learned to rely on God, day by day, for all he had need of.

John G. Lake had tremendous understanding regarding "the law of the spirit of life" that is ours in Christ Jesus. He lived during the time of the bubonic plague, which was so contagious no one wanted to bury those who died, so John Lake and another man began to help.

When they suffered no harm, they were questioned; John Lake allowed germs to be put on his arm; a microscope showed the germs dying, rather than harming him. He attributed that to the Spirit of life dwelling inside him.

> *"For the law of the Spirit of life in Christ Jesus hath made me free from the law of sin and death."* Romans 8:2

We too can pray into Biblical truths such as these, that we might more fully appropriate them in our lives. As we set our hearts on the Lord Jesus Christ, and contemplate His Word, we give it opportunity to sink into our hearts.

"The things of God knoweth no man, but the Spirit of God. Now we have received ... the spirit which is of God; that we might know the things that are freely given to us of God.

"Which things also we speak ... in the words ... which the Holy Ghost teacheth; comparing spiritual things with spiritual ... because they are spiritually discerned." 1 Corinthians 2:11-14

Spiritual things are spiritually discerned, then appropriated into our lives through faith.

"So then faith cometh by hearing, and hearing by the word of God." Romans 10:17

Verses in the New Testament speak of serving God and even facing hardship, "according to His glorious power."

"Strengthened with all might, according to his glorious power, unto all patience and longsuffering with joyfulness." Colossians 1:11

"Be thou partaker of the afflictions of the gospel according to the power of God." 2 Timothy 1:8

"According as his divine power hath given unto us all things that pertain unto life and godliness, through the knowledge of him that hath called us to glory and virtue." 2 Peter 1:3

In Ephesians 1:18-19, Paul prayed that we would experientially know this power: *"The eyes of your understanding being enlightened; that you may know ... what is the exceeding greatness of his power toward us who believe, according to the working of His mighty power."*

Come what may, we do not need to face anything in our own strength; we can live in His strength. With so much uncertainty around us, our comfort and security are in Him. Come what may, we can shelter under the arms of the Almighty God (Psalm 91).

Whatever we face, He will be with us (Hebrews 13:5). Times of joy! Times of sorrow. Times of blessing! Times of testing. He gives us strength to make it through every season, as He also works deep within our hearts.

As we pray into all that is happening, our faith is also laying hold of that which is eternal, that we will know the power of God in our bodies and in our circumstances, that we will be made ready for eternity.

Our prayer is that all those who shelter under the everlasting arms of the Almighty God, will know His power and receive His strength, that together we will be a light and encouragement to others, that others too, may come to know His saving power.

Communion is one of the ways, as believers, the Lord strengthens us. It is one of the ways we receive of His life and healing. As we prayerfully present these truths, our prayer is that you too will receive the blessing that comes when these truths are appropriated in our lives.

As I write especially this portion, my desire has been to honor "the faith of our fathers," and of my dad, who had an impact on my life and on the lives of others. As

I mentioned earlier, the understanding of Communion that grew in his heart was especially special to him and was a part of his daily devotional times.

Because of that, I would like to share "The Lasting Value of Communion" by Wade Taylor, with you as part of this book. It is on our ministry website, where you can read it, copy it, or share it with others freely. I am also including it in the Appendix of this book. May you be blessed through the truths he shares.

Most of all, may you too, find time for times of refreshing in the presence of the Lord, that you may be built up, strengthened, and encouraged through God's Word, as you spend time with Him.

This is our primary calling and our first priority! All else flows from there.

Note:

To read "The Lasting Value of Communion" by Wade Taylor:

See the Appendix in the back of this book.

or,

Go to www.wadetaylor.org.

Scroll down our Menu to "Search."

Type in *The Lasting Value of Communion,* then press Go.

When the Title appears, click on it to read the complete teaching.

To Hear and See a video by Wade Taylor on *"Communion":*

Go to www.wadetaylor.org.

Scroll down our Menu to "Messages to See and Hear."

Select *Communion Teaching.*

Encouragement

"But grow in grace, and in the knowledge of our Lord and Saviour Jesus Christ." 2 Peter 3:18

I am encouraged as the years go by and I see areas of my life where I am not the same person I used to be. Yet there are areas where God is still working in me.

The Bible says *"If any man be in Christ, he is a new creature"* (1 Corinthians 5:17a). If that is so, why do we still have areas in our lives that are less than we would desire?

We are saved by faith (Ephesians 2:8). When I accept Jesus as my Lord and Saviour, instantly, my sins are forgiven. But now we are to *"grow up into Him in all things"* (Ephesians 4:15), or in every aspect of our lives. How do we grow up into Him?

It's the Lord's desire to take us beyond our sin being forgiven, to our nature being changed to become more like Christ. This requires an inner working of the Lord. As we choose to yield to Him, He begins to do this further work in our hearts.

"For it is God which worketh in you both to will and to do of his good pleasure." Philippians 2:13

The Word of God works within us as the Spirit of the Lord changes us. Through a progressive working of the Lord, inner change comes, which then becomes outwardly visible.

Now, the Word of God is no longer just written in stone or on paper, but in my heart (2 Corinthians 3:2-3). His life flows from that Word and by His Spirit changes me:

"But we all ... are changed into the same image from glory to glory, even as by the Spirit of the Lord." 2 Corinthians 3:18

This is a lifelong process of growth which we never outgrow. My salvation is sure; it is Christ that lives in me. Now He is working in me (Romans 8:27-29). We are to become *"as he is"* in this life, because *"as he is, so are we in this world"* (1 John 4:17b).

Paul spoke of himself not as one who had already attained or was already made perfect, but as one who was pressing forward, believing for God's highest and best in his life. Then he said:

> *"Let us therefore, as many as be perfect, be thus minded: and if in any thing ye be otherwise minded, God shall reveal even this unto you."* Philippians 3:15

The apostle Paul realized God was still working in him. How important it is that we see Christ working in us, as areas of our lives are being changed. We need a Saviour, that is why He died for us! We are less than perfect, that is why He works within us. What great love and mercy overshadows our lives!

In John 3:7 Jesus says, *"Marvel not that I say unto you, you must be born again."* Then in Matthew 16:24, *"If any man will come after me, let him deny himself, and take up his cross, and follow me."*

In His first statement, Jesus is talking about sins being forgiven. In His second statement, He is talking about the outworking of the cross in our lives until we are able to say like Paul,

> *"I am crucified with Christ: nevertheless I live; yet not I, but Christ liveth in me."* Galatians 2:20

Salvation is a free gift, but this new nature (or godly character) is not a gift; there is cost involved as I submit my life to the Lord Jesus Christ and allow His working within my life. That power by which Christ rose from the dead, is the same power by which we now can walk in this newness of life.

Initially, as an act of my will, I make choices, then the Lord enables me. I continue to make choices until through those choices my nature is changed, and it becomes no longer just my choice, but who I am.

As I make these choices and I choose to walk in His ways, He delights in me and the progress I am making. What an encouragement!

We can be thankful for all that God has done, as we continue to yield to His working day by day, being sure that He will finish that good work which He has begun in us.

Also encouraging is when we remember areas Christ has brought victory into our lives. The Israelites were taught to remember all the mighty things God had done in the past, and to rehearse them, giving thanks to the Lord.

Our thoughts can be uplifting or pull us down. How worthy the Lord is of our thanksgiving and praise, as we reflect on those things He has already accomplished in our lives.

There were times when David was under great pressure. There was not always someone to encourage him, but he learned to encourage himself in the Lord. We too can learn to do this.

"...but David encouraged himself in the LORD his God." 1 Samuel 30:6

Our faith and hope is in Christ and the finished work of Calvary. It is God who girds us with strength! He gives us hinds' feet! It is He who makes our way perfect.

> *"It is God that girdeth me with strength, and maketh my way perfect. He maketh my feet like hinds' feet, and setteth me upon my high places."* Psalm 18:32–33

John the Baptist said, *"He must increase, but I must decrease"* (John 3:30). As we maintain our focus on Christ and walk in a love relationship with Him, He fills our lives more and more. As He does, that which is not pleasing to Him becomes displaced.

We can be confident as we continue to follow His ways, growing up into Him in all things, that *"...he which hath begun a good work in you will perform it until the day of Jesus Christ"* (Philippians 1:6).

Living With Purpose

"For we are his workmanship, created in Christ Jesus unto good works, which God hath before ordained that we should walk in them." Ephesians 2:10

Billy Graham once said, "Life without God is like an unsharpened pencil – it has no point." In Christ, we not only know who we are, we have a purpose today and a destiny, an expectation for all of eternity.

In 1 Peter 1:23, we understand we are born again of an incorruptible seed, by the word of God. Then, as we begin in our new walk with the Lord, we are to mature and grow (1 Peter 2:2; 2 Peter 3:18).

Through the choices I make, a process of sanctification begins. That which is not like Christ begins to fall away as I receive His enabling grace in my life. When I choose the Lord and His ways, I am changed, until it is no longer my old nature ruling my life, but now Christ within (Galatians 2:20).

We are excited when God works in our lives during pleasant times! But it is sometimes hard to see anything of value during difficult times, or even to maintain a right attitude so our lives can be a testimony to others, without an understanding of the working of the Lord and this process of transformation.

As I yield to the Lord in every season, submitting myself to Him and His inner working, Christ is interceding for me, and I have the promise of a "working together for good," that I might be conformed into the image of His Son (Ephesians 2:10; Romans 8:26-29; 2 Peter 1:4). To know this, gives me strength and comfort and adds meaning to what otherwise might seem futile or mundane.

Though at times we see only our present circumstances, as we learn to live from an eternal perspective, we can find rest in the fact that *"it is God which worketh in (me) both to will and to do of his good pleasure"* (Philippians 2:13).

If we have made Him Lord of our lives, we are in His hands! As we continue to submit our lives to Him, and yield, allowing His working to take place inside us, we are strengthened to stand, for come what may, our hope, faith, trust, and destiny is in Him.

> *"The LORD is my strength and my shield; my heart trusteth in him, and I am helped: therefore my heart greatly rejoiceth; and with my song I will praise him."* Psalm 28:7

2 Corinthians 3:3 speaks of our calling to be "epistles of Christ," written with the Spirit of the living God. Again, our lives are the only Bible some people will ever read! It's not God's will that any should perish.

God has always had a witness! As carriers of His presence and reflectors of His truth, today we have the privilege of sharing Him with others through our lives, even when our words cannot speak.

The Lord is raising up a people who in every circumstance have the grace to "be" a witness and a testimony unto Him (Acts 1:8). Even in the midst of great darkness, His glory is shining forth through an overcoming people who have put their trust in Him.

As Christ showed forth the glory of the Father in the midst of great darkness, may we too show forth His glory as an overcoming, end time people, appointed and anointed to be carriers of His presence, ordained to be faithful witnesses unto Him in our day. A people who are not just hearers, but doers of His Word; a people through whom Christ in all His power and glory can move today (Isaiah 60:1-2).

2 Thessalonians 1:10 speaks of Christ coming back "to be admired in His saints." Paul speaks of this as a great mystery, that which had been hid, but is now made manifest to the Lord's people. This is our calling! Our hope! Our joy! (Colossians 1:26-27).

A verse the National Day of Prayer task force chose one year is a wonderful admonition and encouragement to each one of us as we continue on, day by day, with our daily lives. In light of all that has gone on in the past and all that is happening today, what a timely word for each of us!

"So then, just as you received Christ Jesus as Lord, continue to live your lives in him, rooted and built up in him, strengthened in the faith as you were taught, and overflowing with thankfulness." Colossians 2:6-7 NIV

May this be our posture as we continue in our walk with the Lord, being faithful in those things He has called us to do.

Maintaining Focus

"Who hath ... called us with an holy calling ... according to his own purpose and grace, which was given us in Christ Jesus before the world began." 2 Timothy 1:9

Because of God's promise to him, King David prayed that his son, Solomon, would have a perfect heart, that he might build a house for the Lord. David imparted vision to his son, speaking prophetically into his life, causing Solomon to understand his calling – what the Lord desired, and his role in the fulfillment of the Lord's desire.

As a result, when Solomon became king, he responded in three outstanding ways to the instruction he had received regarding building a house for the Lord: (1) he made a decision; (2) he started; and (3) he finished!

"And Solomon <u>determined</u> to build an house for the name of the LORD." 2 Chronicles 2:1a

"Then Solomon <u>began</u> to build the house of the LORD at Jerusalem in mount Moriah, where the LORD appeared unto David his father." 2 Chronicles 3:1a

"Thus all the work that Solomon made for the house of the LORD was <u>finished</u>." 2 Chronicles 5:1a

When Solomon first became king, he prayed, *"Now, O LORD God, let thy promise to David my father be established: for thou hast made me king over a people like the dust of the earth in multitude"* (2 Chronicles 1:9).

After Solomon had finished building the house for the Lord, he then prayed again, dedicating to the Lord all that had been done. He sought the Lord's blessing and manifest presence to be in the place he had built for Him. The Lord was pleased and answered the desire of Solomon's heart.

"Now when Solomon had made an end of praying, the fire came down from heaven, and consumed the burnt offering and the

sacrifices; and the glory of the LORD filled the house." 2 Chronicles 7:1

Paul encourages us to offer our lives to the Lord as a sacrifice, pure and holy.

"I beseech you therefore, brethren, by the mercies of God, that ye present your bodies a living sacrifice, holy, acceptable unto God." Romans 12:1

In the Old Testament, when a sacrifice was accepted by the Lord, it was consumed with fire. In the New Testament, John the Baptist said:

"I indeed baptize you with water unto repentance: but he that cometh after me is mightier than I, whose shoes I am not worthy to bear: he shall baptize you with the Holy Ghost, and with fire." Matthew 3:11

Jesus is coming to be glorified in His saints and to be seen and admired through the lives of those who believe (2 Thessalonians 1:10). As we let our own lives be consumed, allowing the fire of His presence to burn within us, then it is Jesus who is seen, His purpose fulfilled, and His heart satisfied in and through our lives.

One of my favorite songs: "For I was born to be thy dwelling place, a home for the presence of the Lord. So let my life now be separated, Lord, to thee, that I might be what I was born to be."

We are called to "be" or "become" a "place" built for the Lord, dedicated to the Lord, and marked by His presence. Our testimony to others occurs simply when it is Jesus (rather than our Adamic nature) who is seen and admired through our lives.

> *"I am crucified with Christ: nevertheless I live; yet not I, but Christ liveth in me."* Galatians 2:20a

> *"He must increase, but I must decrease."* John 3:30

In the busyness of each day, it is so important that we maintain a clear vision of that which our Lord has called us to and that we stay faithful to that vision.

Solomon could have done many other things, but he sought the Lord's enablement, asked for wisdom, and gave himself to the call of God on his life, not only beginning, but finishing that which he set out to do.

Focus and priority! Human tendency is to make grand New Year's resolutions and begin new projects with great zeal. Yet, how determined are we to stay true to those things we know the Lord has called us to?

Are we taking decisive steps toward that which God has called us as we look to Him for His divine enablement? Do we not only begin, but finish with determination and steadfastness?

"Jesus saith unto them, My meat is to do the will of him that sent me, and to finish his work." John 4:34

From scripture, we know that Solomon's life did not end as well as it began. He personally could have attained to more if he had allowed God to deal with particular areas in his own life. Even so, he fulfilled the call imparted to him to build a place for the presence of the Lord, and in that, the Lord was pleased.

May our life commitment be not only to *begin* each task well, but also to *finish* our lives well, that we might be able to say as Paul said concerning his call, *"I was not disobedient unto the heavenly vision"* (Acts 26:19).

Our goal is to be able to say, not only at the end of each assignment God gives us, but at the end of our lives here on earth, *"I have fought a good fight, I have finished my course, I have kept the faith"* (2 Timothy 4:7).

Believing God

"Now the just shall live by faith." Hebrews 10:38

As I've been looking at the book of James again, I am reminded that it is a very practical book. Its message has to do with believing God, then putting our faith into action!

The words "faith" and "works" each are mentioned sixteen times in James' writing. We can't be saved simply by doing good things. The only way to heaven is through faith in the Lord Jesus Christ. But if you do believe in Jesus, and if He is Lord of your life, it will be evidenced by the things you do.

"Even so faith, if it hath not works, is dead, being alone." James 2:17

Our faith is shown by our decisions, by the things we say, the way we live, the choices we make. Faith is evidenced by our prayers, continuance in prayer, and our seeking the Lord's counsel.

Hard times or good times, our faces are to be turned toward the Lord in faith and expectation. God has a plan. A purpose! We can be as doors through whom the Lord can move, windows through whom He can be seen.

I am always encouraged by the life of Abraham. He faced famine, strife, and war, fearing for his life at times. He dealt with family problems and employee problems. Rather than settling in a comfortable home, he faced the difficulties of travel, walking the land as he had been instructed by God (Genesis 12:1; Genesis 13:12-17).

Through all this, Abraham considered not the circumstances, but believed that what God had promised, He was able to do, and it was counted to him for righteousness (Romans 4:3; 17-22).

Abraham was faithful in his everyday responsibilities, sought guidance at intersections in his walk, and trusted God with his life right through to his old age.

He was a worshipper! A man of prayer. A man of faith! He was called a friend of God (James 2:23).

Noteworthy, is that often when God spoke of His promise to Abraham, it was when Abraham was simply worshipping the Lord. As he ministered to the Lord, the Lord would then talk to Abraham not only about what He was doing, but also about Abraham's own life.

True faith results in worship and brings a rest in God. He is God! The Lord God Almighty! We are not! As we rest in Him, He is able to speak, stir, and move in whatever way He desires, when He desires! From a quietness of heart, we can better hear, receive, and respond.

When the Lord looks at the earth, may He find faith! (Luke 18:8). Our faith! Faith in every nation, tongue, tribe, and people.

A people of faith are being gathered from every nation, around the throne to worship Him. Revelation 22:2 speaks of the throne and the tree of life whose leaves are for the healing of the nations.

"And they sung a new song, saying, Thou art worthy to take the book, and to open the seals thereof: for thou wast slain, and hast redeemed us to God by thy blood out of every kindred, and tongue, and people, and nation." Revelation 5:9

May the Lord's desire be fulfilled as, together, we become an active part of that which He is doing today.

"Arise, shine; for thy light is come, and the glory of the LORD is risen upon thee. For, behold, the darkness shall cover the earth, and gross darkness the people: but the LORD shall arise upon thee, and his glory shall be seen upon thee." Isaiah 60:1-2

May we too walk in the ways of the Lord, as ones with whom the Lord can share His heart.

May our faith be marked by integrity, worship, and fellowship with the Lord.

Even as Christ showed forth the glory of the Father, may we too show forth His glory as an overcoming, end time people, appointed and anointed to be carriers of His presence; ordained to be faithful witnesses unto Him in the day in which we live.

May God's purposes move forward, even as they did in Abraham's day, through a people who believe God in spite of circumstances and are persuaded that what He has promised, He is able to perform.

A Commitment to the Lord

"My voice shalt thou hear in the morning, O LORD; in the morning will I direct my prayer unto thee, and will look up." Psalm 5:3

The "parousia" of the Lord speaks of the "presencing" of the Lord which precedes the second coming of Christ. The Lord is raising up a people "of His presence" today as a witness or sample of the Lord Jesus Christ, that His presence might be made known, so others too might come to see and know Christ.

We are called to "be" a witness (Acts 1:8). The Lord is coming to be glorified and admired "in" His people (2 Thessalonians 1:10). He is inviting us to become "joined" with Him in who He is and what He is doing today. There is no greater fellowship or fulfillment in this life than our personal relationship with the Lord Jesus Christ.

Psalm 42:7 speaks of "deep calling unto deep." The deep in the heart of God is calling out to the deep inside of us, that we might come to know Him in a deeper way, fellowshipping with Him in His purposes.

I have learned there is no better way for a relationship to deepen than to spend time together. Your relationship grows as you spend time together in the normal activities of life, and that is good. But you also need quality times together away from the daily routine, where things on your heart that otherwise might not have been shared, can find expression.

In our walk with the Lord, we are to practice His presence, living every moment of every day in fellowship with Him. Yet we also need quality times of fellowship away from the busyness of life. Both dimensions of "time together" are vital to a growing relationship.

I like to start each day in fellowship with the Lord. One of the first things I do each morning is talk with the Lord, whether by giving thanks, expressing worship, asking for wisdom, or praying for someone on my heart. I can't imagine starting my day any other way, as I consecrate the day to Him.

However, I believe Psalm 5:3 can also be applied in another way. "Morning" can speak not just of a time of day, but of making the Lord the first priority in our lives. Not when all else fails, we seek Him; but first, as a lifestyle, and the way we think and live.

What time of day are you free to prioritize your time? Is it after the kids are off to school? Or when you first come home from work? Maybe it is first thing in the morning! Or in the evening, when you can finally settle down for some quiet moments before going to sleep.

Day by day, may we find that time and prioritize our fellowship with the Lord. From these times may the Lord touch, bless, and fill you with a fresh anointing, that you might be strengthened, encouraged, and empowered, to walk in His ways with increased understanding, purpose, and joy.

The preparation of a people for the end time purposes of the Lord! The establishing of places marked by the presence of the Lord! It begins in our prayer closets, and day by day continues to flow from there.

May we be a part of that people who He is raising up today, those whose lives are marked by His presence. May we become carriers of His presence, "joined" with Him in who He is and what He is doing today.

> "*My voice shalt thou hear in the morning, O LORD; in the morning will I direct my prayer unto thee, and will look up.*" Psalm 5:3

As we take time to fellowship with the Lord in a deeper way we will never regret it.

Final Thoughts

As I come to the close of this book, the second in this *Spiritual Food for Spiritual Growth* series, I think again of what, for me, was the beginning.

In 1981 the Lord called me to support my dad, Wade Taylor, in what he was doing. Later, I realized it was not just to support a person, but a vision – the preparation of a people for the end time purposes of the Lord – and it burns deep in my heart today.

My writings sow into that vision. They express truths that changed my life and are now deeply embedded in my heart, life, and walk with the Lord today.

This is my prayer for you also; that your life will be enriched as you consider these truths and that they will become part of your life experience. Each one of us who has dedicated our life to the Lord is enrolled in a "school of the spirit." The classroom is our life experiences, as we apply the Word of God and seek His heart.

Through the years, as I have been writing, it has been my desire that the writings would help draw each one into a closer relationship with the Lord; that each one would be encouraged to spend their own time with the Lord and be strengthened in their own walk with Him; apprehending that for which they have been apprehended.

In making these books available, this continues to be my desire, that these writings will encourage you in your own personal relationship with the Lord and times apart with Him. That you will recognize in a greater way, His working within you, and be encouraged by all God has done, is doing, and will yet do.

Much emphasis has been placed on the individual and on each person's individual walk with the Lord. However, may we always realize we are part of a corporate body. Our relationships are very important and part of God's plan. It's together, that our calls will be fulfilled and God's purposes accomplished.

Thank you for taking the time to read these books. May our Lord bless you through that which has been shared. May the scriptures linger in your heart. If they are there to remember, the Holy Spirit will bring them to mind as you need them!

Today is the day we have to make choices. There is a preparation that is taking place in each of our lives. My prayer is that as the five wise virgins, we too, may be found ready at the time of His appearing. May Christ be seen and glorified in our lives. May we too, be partakers together with Him in that which He is yet about to do.

Blessing

As we conclude Book Two of the *Spiritual Food for Spiritual Growth* series, we again speak this blessing over your life. This is a blessing that was first spoken by my dad, Wade Taylor. We continue to speak this same blessing:

May you increasingly prosper, both

spiritually and in your life circumstances,

beyond all that you have experienced in the

past, and also, may you be blessed in life, in

health, and in all that is before you.

Prayerfully yours,

Nancy Taylor Tate

Parousia Ministries
www.wadetaylor.org

Appendix

The Lasting Value of Communion

Wade E. Taylor

As the *"facets"* in a diamond are viewed, some appear as being opposite to other facets. The beauty of a diamond is due to the fact that these *"opposite"* facets complement each other. So also, the partaking of *"communion"* with our Lord has many different ways in which it can be understood and experienced.

Some receive communion in a ritualistic manner, by partaking of a symbol, or emblem of the Lord's body and blood. There is no life in a symbol or emblem and these receive only a religious or sentimental satisfaction.

Others recognize that they are partaking of the very life of the Lord, and as they partake, they are receiving His literal body and blood being imparted into them.

There should be a time of preparation so we can effectively partake of *"communion."* We must be lifted into the presence of the Lord in order for His life to flow into our lives. Just as it is not possible for us to *"wait on the Lord in His presence"* until we have passed from the natural realm into the spiritual, it is not possible for us to *"receive"* the literal body and blood of Jesus, until we exchange realms.

The word *"communion"* has to do with communication – Jesus speaks and we listen, then we speak and He listens. Thus, when we enter into *"communion"* with Jesus and become *"one"* with Him, as being a *"branch"* that is properly attached to the *"vine,"* we are able to partake of His life.

There are foundational principles that are established in the Word of God, which apply to our partaking of communion.

> *"There is therefore now no condemnation to them which are in Christ Jesus ... For the law of the Spirit of Life in Christ Jesus has made me free from the law of sin and death."*
> Romans 8:1-2

This *"condemnation"* is the judgment (*death*) that was imparted to Adam for his transgression. This judgment of death has been handed down to each of us. Jesus shed His blood on the cross that we might be redeemed. Through our acceptance of the salvation that He has provided, we are set free from the *"law of sin."* Through our participation in the resurrection and ascension of Jesus, we are set free from the *"law of death."*

We become a partaker of the *"law of the Spirit of Life in Christ Jesus"* through our identification with Jesus as being a quickening, life-giving Spirit.

"And so it is written, The first man Adam was made a living soul; the last Adam (Jesus) was made a quickening (life-giving) spirit." 1 Corinthians 15:45

This includes healing, divine health, and longevity of life. Those who receive this gift of *"life"* from Jesus will stand out from all others in the quality of their health, and the length of their life span.

Jesus fed the multitude with five loaves and two fishes. Later, when they again became hungry, they returned to ask for more. Jesus told them that He had something better for them, and said:

"Except you eat the flesh of the Son of Man, and drink His blood, you have no life in you ... Your fathers did eat manna, and are dead: he that eats of this bread shall live forever." John 6:53, 58

Jesus offered them a higher life in which they would not die. The condition being that they eat, not a second serving of loaves and fishes, but rather, His very flesh and blood. This word concerning our *"living forever"* primarily applies to our eternal life in heaven, but there is a present application of this that can affect us in our present life. Jesus said:

> *"I am the true vine ... Abide in Me, and I in you. As the branch cannot bear fruit of itself, except it abide in the vine; no more can you, except you abide in Me. I am the vine, you are the branches: He that abides in Me, and I in him, the same brings forth much fruit: for without Me you can do nothing."* John 15:1-5

Jesus said that He is the *"vine"* (*Tree of Life*), and that we, as being a branch, only have life as we partake of His life. Through Adam's transgression, we were removed from our connection to the Tree of Life, and became attached to the tree of knowledge.

The Lord slew an animal and covered Adam and Eve with its skin, which through the shedding of blood, resulted in forgiveness. Adam and Eve were forgiven, but they still had within them that which they ate from the tree of knowledge, the right to choose for themselves – they lost their abiding state of dependence on the Lord and could no longer partake of the Tree of Life.

Therefore, each one of us was born attached to the tree of knowledge. Through the total victory that Jesus gained in our behalf on the cross, we can detach ourselves from the tree of knowledge and re-attach ourselves to the Tree of Life. Then as we *"partake of communion,"* we receive the very life of Jesus flowing directly into us.

If we partake of communion as being a symbol or emblem, we are partaking of a dead religious form. Jesus is no longer dead, but He was resurrected from death and has ascended to the throne to be seated on the right hand of His Father.

Thus, the bread is <u>living</u> bread turned into His <u>living</u> body. The cup, the fruit of the vine, turned into His blood, is His <u>living</u> blood. As we partake, His life is being imparted into us, so He can live His life through us.

If a strip of bark is totally cut around a tree and removed, the process of death will begin. The tree can no longer receive the life that is drawn up from the root system, and will soon die. So also, the life of the "*Vine*" (*Jesus*) is to flow into us, as being a "*branch*" that is attached to the "*Vine.*" For this to take place, the branch (*us*) must be properly connected to the vine. Only then can the life of Jesus, as being the "*power of an endless life*," flow into us.

Therefore, each morning when I arise, one of the first things I do is as follows:

"Lord, I thank you for a good night's rest. Lord, through Adam's transgression, I was born attached to the tree of knowledge. But through your redemption in my behalf, I release myself from being attached to the tree of knowledge, and as being a branch, I humbly come to the true vine, and I re-attach myself to the Tree of Life, so your life can flow into my life, as I partake of your living body, and your living blood."

Eating food to sustain our natural body is a necessity and, we eat several times each day. Also, our "*partaking*" of the life of Jesus is not an option. This partaking of the living "*body*" and "*blood*" of Jesus should take place more often than the Church practice of partaking of communion on the first Sunday of each month. Rather, we should partake daily, or we will suffer loss, both spiritually and naturally.

> *"And the Lord God said, Behold, the man is become as one of us, to know good and evil: and now, lest he put forth his hand, and take also of the tree of life, and eat, and live forever."* Genesis 3:22

I once thought that Adam had eternal existence built within him at the time of his creation, and that he would have lived forever if he had not transgressed. However, Adam had been formed from *"dust,"* which speaks of a created dependency. It is impossible to form anything from dust. It takes *"moisture,"* the very life of our Lord Jesus Christ – that which flows from the Vine into the *"dust"* that we are, in order for us to have form, shape, and purpose.

"Lest he put forth his hand and take also of the tree of life, and eat, and live forever" (Genesis 3:22). Adam

came regularly and partook, and as a result, he continued to live, but when he transgressed, he was hindered from partaking of the Tree of Life (*taking communion*), and he began to die. When we take communion, we "*put forth our hand and we take and eat.*" Suddenly, I saw what was being said:

Had Adam been able to continue to eat of the Tree of Life, he would have continued to live, but the judgment for transgression was death. All that the Lord needed to do to fulfill this judgment was to prevent Adam from taking communion (*putting forth his hand ... taking ... eating, and living*). Therefore, the Lord placed an angel with a flaming sword before the Tree of Life, to prevent Adam from partaking.

On the day of Pentecost, this "*flaming sword*" was removed from being a hindrance, and became a means of access. This flaming sword descended and sat upon the head of each of the one-hundred-twenty who were present, and they were filled with the Holy Spirit. The veil had been rent, and a way of access made for us to enter the Lord's presence.

"To him that overcomes will I give to eat of the tree of life, which is in the midst of the paradise of God." Revelation 2:7

As we partake of *"communion,"* the way of entrance to the Tree of Life is opened to us, and we can partake of the very life of Jesus, as He is the Tree of Life.

When the multitude, who came to see miracles, became hungry, Jesus multiplied five loaves and two fishes, and they were fed to the full (John 6:1-26). Later, they came back for more, and when Jesus told them that they were to eat His flesh and drink His blood, they ridiculed Him and left. At that time, Jesus could not explain how to partake of His flesh and drink His blood, as it was not yet time for Him to die upon the cross for our sin, and then in resurrection, become to us quickening life-giving spirit.

When the time of Jesus' ministry was completed, during the evening before He was to give His life on the cross, He was able to explain how we are to eat His flesh and drink His blood.

"... the Lord Jesus ... took bread: and when He had given thanks, He broke it, and said, Take, eat: this is My body, which is broken for you: this do in remembrance of Me. After the same manner also He took the cup, when He had supped, saying, This cup is the new testament in My blood: this do you, as often as you drink it, in remembrance of Me." 1 Corinthians 11:23-25

Notice that Jesus said, *"This bread is My body; and, this cup is My blood."* He did not say, *"This is an emblem, or a symbol of My body and of My blood."* Jesus then said that He would not partake again with us until we partook together with Him, in the Kingdom.

"For I say to you, I will not any more eat thereof, until it be fulfilled in the kingdom of God." Luke 22:16

The Word says, *"Unless you are converted and become as little children, you will by no means enter the kingdom of heaven"* (Matthew 18:3). When we partake of communion, we see bread, but Jesus said, *"This is My body."* As we partake of the cup, we see the fruit of the vine, but Jesus said, *"This is My blood."* Having the mind of a child, we are to simply believe what Jesus said – not what we see.

Some teach that the *"bread,"* and the *"fruit of the vine,"* must first be transformed into the body and the blood of Jesus, and a priest seeks to do this for the believer. Others say that we can do this for ourselves, without the priest.

Rather, we are to believe what Jesus said, and partake of the bread and the fruit of the vine in faith, believing that we are partaking of the literal body and blood of Jesus. The necessary change is in *"us,"* not in the bread and the fruit of the vine.

> *"And when He had given thanks, He broke it, and said, Take, eat: this is My body, which is broken for you: this do in remembrance of Me. After the same manner also He took the cup, when He had supped, saying, This cup is the new testament in My blood: this do*

> *you, as often as you drink it, in remembrance*
> *of Me."* 1 Corinthians 11:24-25

"This do you, as often as you drink it..." This word *"often"* clearly says we can personally partake of communion as often as we desire. We are totally free to partake anytime. We are not limited to communion being served in a church service.

Jesus said that we are to partake *"in remembrance of Me."* Rather than referring to our remembering His death on the cross, He is directing our thoughts back to the time when He told the multitude that they were to *"eat His flesh and drink His blood."*

> *"From that time many of His disciples went*
> *back, and walked no more with Him. Then*
> *said Jesus to the twelve, Will you also go*
> *away?"* John 6:66-67

At that time, Jesus could not explain how to partake, but now, He could. With this understanding, when we believe what Jesus said, with child-like faith, we are literally partaking of His body and blood. As we partake, we must make a decision – *"Lord, I look and*

I see bread and the fruit of the vine, but I choose to believe, not what I see, but what you said" (*this is My body, and My blood*).

> *"And so it is written, The first man Adam was made a living soul; the last Adam was made a quickening (living, life-giving) spirit."* 1 Corinthians 15:45

In His ascension, Jesus became available to us as a life-giving Spirit, as He is the Tree of Life.

> *"Who is made, not after the law of a carnal commandment, but after the power of an endless life."* Hebrews 7:16

Thus, when we partake of communion, we are eating and drinking the very life of the One who is able to impart life.

> *"For He shall grow up before Him as a tender plant, and as a root out of a dry ground."* Isaiah 53:2

Jesus is a *"root"* (*the Tree of Life*) out of a dry ground. Therefore, it can be said that He is the Tree of Life in mystical form, recognizable only to those who have spiritual eyes.

> *"But let a man examine himself, and so let him eat of that bread, and drink of that cup. For he that eats and drinks unworthily, eats and drinks damnation to himself, not discerning the Lord's body. For this cause many are weak and sickly among you, and many sleep."* 1 Corinthians 11:28-30

Communion is the *"mystical form"* of the Tree of Life, hidden from the spiritually blind. Jesus said that if we partake unworthily (*without understanding that He Himself is the Tree of Life*), we are merely partaking of the process of death, receiving bread and the fruit of the vine – another good meal and we are that much closer to death.

But, if we partake with spiritual understanding, knowing what we are doing, we will no longer be weak, sickly, and dying prematurely. Rather, as we rightly partake of communion, we are receiving "quickening life-giving spirit," and we will be living.

> *"For as often as you eat this bread, and drink this cup, you do show the Lord's death till He come."* 1 Corinthians 11:26

"For as often as you eat...." This tells us that we can personally, privately partake of communion, whenever we choose to do so. Our *"showing"* the Lord's death means that we are demonstrating the value of it. If we die the same as other people, we are not demonstrating anything. When we partake of life, we are receiving the life that Jesus came to offer – *"Life more abundantly."*

Paul tells us that we have been set free from the *"law of sin and death."* As we identify with Jesus in His death on the cross, and then partake of the bread (*His body*), we receive healing and we are released from the process of death.

We then identify with Jesus in His resurrection and ascension. As He ascended, He became *"quickening spirit."* In this identification, we receive the life of Jesus as the life of the vine flowing into us as being a branch. Then, His life can be lived within us.

Thus, we are partaking *"worthily."*

The *"Tree of Life"* relates to life or death. The *"tree of the knowledge of good and evil"* relates to that which is good or bad, or, right or wrong. In our daily life experiences we often make decisions, or choices that relate to right or wrong, and comment about it being either good or bad. As we do this, we again become attached to the tree of knowledge.

Therefore, as I prepare for communion, the first thing I do is to release myself from this attachment to the Tree of Knowledge. I then reattach myself to the Tree of Life and speak to the Lord words that include the following:

"Lord, I release the totality of my being from the Tree of Knowledge, and through your redemption in my behalf, I humbly come to you and reattach myself to the Tree of Life, as being a branch that can live, only as I receive the life of the true vine, flowing into my life.

Lord, you took bread and blessed it as being your body. Lord, I sanctify this bread that I am holding in my hand, to be what you said it is, your body. As I partake, I receive your living body being imparted into the totality of my being, that you might live your life within my life.

Lord, you then took the cup and blessed it as being your blood. Lord, I sanctify this cup, the fruit of the vine, that I am holding in my hand, to be what you said it is, your living blood. And as I partake, I receive your living blood, the power of an endless life, so your body can actively live within my life.

Lord, in identification with you as being the Tree of Life, I release the totality of my being from the power of death, and I receive healing and longevity of life, that you might live your life through my life."

Just as Adam, we must come often to the "*Tree of Life*" in order to continue to live, or we will progressively die. Therefore, when we, in faith, partake of communion as being the "*Tree of Life*," we will live the fullness of the time that has been given to us.

Those whom the Lord is calling to become "*remaining ones*" are discovering the connection between communion and the Tree of Life as a principle that is being revealed at the present time. Paul said, *"We who are alive and remain at the coming of the Lord..."* (1 Thessalonians 4:15).

Jesus, on the eighth day of His life, was taken into the temple to be dedicated. Two people were there, Anna and Simeon. Anna was old, but Simeon had a *"word"* that he would not see death until he saw the anointed of the Lord. Anna was *"alive,"* but Simeon was *"remaining."* Thus, two classes of people were present.

Paul said that in the time of the return of our Lord, these two classes would be present; those who are *"alive"* through the normal course of life, and those who are *"remaining"* - whose lives have been extended because they have learned the principle of communion.

These are looking beyond liturgical religious forms, into spiritual reality and are partaking in faith, knowing that they are eating the very flesh, and drinking the very blood of Jesus, who is the Tree of Life.

Communion can be taken as often as we desire. The Word clearly confirms this – "*As often as you eat this bread, and drink this cup, you show the Lord's death (demonstrate the value, by receiving life), till He come*" (1 Corinthians 11:26).

If we realize that we are partaking of healing and life, we will do so, often.

Books by
Nancy Taylor Tate

That I Might Know Him

Spiritual Food for Spiritual Growth – Book One

Walking In His Ways

Spiritual Food for Spiritual Growth – Book Two

For More Deeper Life Teachings:

Please visit our ministry website, www.wadetaylor.org.

For Ministry Contact:

Please visit our ministry website, www.wadetaylor.org,
for our contact information.

Made in United States
North Haven, CT
26 December 2022

30170886R00137